Acknowledgements:

We would like to thank the following for their co-operation and support in the preparation of this report: Professor James Arthur, Dr John Collier, Dr Ruth Deakin Crick, Dr Ken Dickens, Professor Leslie Francis, Professor Gerald Grace, Dr Arthur Jones, Dr Bill Lattimer, Dr Andrew Morris, Dr John Shortt and Professor David Smith. We are also grateful to Geoff Lawson from the *Transforming Lives* Steering Group for an insightful piece of advice and to Heather Miller from the Stapleford Centre for her hard work on proofreading. Responsibility for the opinions expressed remains with the authors alone as do any errors or omissions.

Theos

The public theology think tank

what Theos is

Theos is a public theology think tank which exists to undertake research and provide commentary on social and political arrangements. We aim to impact opinion around issues of faith and belief in society. We were launched in November 2006 with the support of the Archbishop of Canterbury, Dr Rowan Williams, and the Cardinal Archbishop of Westminster, Cardinal Cormac Murphy-O'Connor. Our first report *"Doing God": A Future for Faith in the Public Square* examined the reasons why faith will play an increasingly significant role in public life.

what Theos stands for

Society is embarking on a process of de-secularisation. Interest in spirituality is increasing across Western culture. Faith is on the agenda of both government and the media. In the arts, humanities and social sciences there are important intellectual developments currently taking place around questions of values and identity. Theos speaks into this new context. Our perspective is that faith is not just important for human flourishing and the renewal of society, but that society can only truly flourish if faith is given the space to do so. We reject notions of a sacred-secular divide.

what Theos works on

Theos undertakes research across a wide range of subject areas. We analyse social and political change and offer interesting new angles and alternative perspectives on the issues that matter.

what Theos provides

Theos provides:

- a research and publishing programme,
- conferences, seminars and lectures,
- outreach to university, college and school students,
- news, information and analysis to media companies and other opinion formers, with a one-stop information line available to journalists,
- regular email bulletins,
- other related activities.

In addition to our independently driven work, Theos provides research, analysis and advice to individuals and organisations across the private, public and not-for-profit sectors. Our unique position within the think tank sector means that we have the capacity to develop proposals that carry values - with an eye to demonstrating what really works. Our staff and consultants have strong public affairs experience, an excellent research track record and a high level of theological literacy. We are practised in campaigning, media relations, detailed policy development and effecting policy change.

www.theosthinktank.co.uk

Mapping the field

A review of the current research evidence on the impact of schools with a Christian ethos

Researcher: **Dr Elizabeth Green**
Research Supervisor: **Dr Trevor Cooling**

Published by Theos in 2009
© Theos

ISBN: 978-0-9562182-0-9

For further information and subscription details please contact:

Theos
Licence Department
34 Buckingham Palace Road
London
SW1W 0RE
United Kingdom

T 020 7828 7777
F hello@theosthinktank.co.uk
www.theosthinktank.co.uk

contents

foreword

faith schools are in the news

During the ten years when Tony Blair was Prime Minister, he strongly advocated an expansion of faith schools. Faith schools were seen as having a special ethos that helped the students within them to develop positive moral and spiritual values and to succeed academically. Government financial support was given to both mainstream Christian organisations and to minority religious groups such as Muslims and Sikhs to build and run their own schools. But what is the evidence for the success of faith schools? Do they really have the advantages claimed for them?

This extensive and careful review of the relevant academic research literature sets out to assess the available evidence on the spiritual impact of schools with a Christian ethos. Dr Elizabeth Green has conducted a comprehensive review of the best evidence available on this question. The resulting report moves the debate on from ideological positionings and presents a fair assessment of what is currently known.

She finds that the evidence supports the claim that students at Roman Catholic and Church of England maintained schools and independent schools with a Christian ethos generally report a more positive attitude towards religion and better spiritual health. Also, while the effect is small, the evidence presented supports the claim that students at maintained church schools gain higher academic achievement beyond the differences that can be accounted for by the measurable prior academic achievement and socio-economic status of the intakes.

But the report also concludes that the currently available research is limited, and does not allow any definitive conclusions to be drawn about the spiritual impact on students of a school's Christian ethos. One of the most important conclusions to this report is that there is a distinct and pressing need for further research on the impact of a Christian school's ethos on students' beliefs, attitudes, behaviour and spiritual development.

This is an important report that deserves to be read by all those interested in the faith schools debate. Its conclusions need to be acted upon.

Geoffrey Walford
Professor of Education Policy,
University of Oxford.

It should strike us as extraordinary that the institution that has sponsored and nurtured education the longest (even more than any government or monarch) should be required to make the case for why it should be involved in public education today. Long before the first universities in the West, the Church through its cathedral schools was the progenitor of education and schooling. There was no England or Europe until languages were given a script and until oral histories were written down; in a word, until schools began.

The Church was at the centre of that cultural formation not because, as secularists assume, the church wished only to proselytise but because at the heart of Christian faith is the holy text and this text from its original Greek and Hebrew scripts was translated into the languages and the dialects of ordinary people. The cultural impact of Wycliffe's and Tyndale's work of translating the Bible into English was as seminal and revolutionary as the impact that Luther's translating the Bible into a dialect of German had in forming the German nation.

Illiterate priests were taught Latin so that they could read the Scriptures which in turn fostered so much of the early medieval cultural renewal of what was to become Western Europe. The steeples on our cathedrals, therefore, are not merely a symbol of the religious moorings of Western European culture; they are also symbols of how Europe came to be civilised.

With our society afflicted by historical myopia, church schools, for example, have had in the last twenty years to justify why they should exist. What culturally should be self evident has now to be restated since many of those who form the media and academic elites seem unaware of their history or are hell-bent on creating a brave new world 'in their own image' – children themselves of a fragmented, individualistic society that emerged after the world wars with its rejection of authority including religion. That this attitude has led to numerous social and educational problems with which we daily struggle seems not to have affected that determination. (This was the thinking in the sixties and seventies that replaced many Victorian buildings with ambitious structures in mortar and aluminium but which today are eye-sores on our city landscapes needing to be pulled down barely thirty years later.)

The sixties and seventies spawned a view about secularity and freedom from the past that has gained credibility by repetition; and religion and the Church have become increasingly marginalised in the public square. Somehow this view anticipates better education without faith or the churches where a form of neutral objectivity exists and children make choices like choosing from a supermarket shelf. (We know that even that simple choice is not uninformed or neutral.) The public square is now dominated by lobbies that use myriad ways to justify their correctness - arguments about human rights, inclusivity, diversity, and even social cohesion, none of which is unacceptable - but often religion is made to look archaic, irrelevant or absurd.

So the case has to be restated again and again not because the church needs to be defensive or self-protective but because of this historical short-sightedness and the state of our educational system greatly in need of wholeness.

This Report does all of us in education a great service in beginning to restate that case – it rightly starts with the links between religiosity and educational attitudes and achievement. Its recommendations to pursue this enquiry further should be taken seriously by all who work within church schools but especially by those in whose hands lies the power to restore and maintain a strong educational system in the United Kingdom. We must not be complacent about that task. To fail will be culturally disastrous and will see the demise of what used to be one of the best educational systems in the world.

Gerald Pillay
Vice-Chancellor,
Liverpool Hope University

introduction

This report is jointly commissioned by Theos and The Stapleford Centre. It was compiled between 16 March and 15 May 2009. The aim of the report is to summarise and evaluate the current research evidence on the impact of primary and secondary schools with a Christian ethos. The review focuses on schools in England and Wales but also draws on a small sample of the wider international literature. It was anticipated that the Christian ethos of a school has the potential to impact the attainment, beliefs, attitudes, behaviours and spiritual development of pupils. It is important to acknowledge that individual teachers may also develop a distinctively Christian ethos in their classrooms capable of impacting pupils. Most of the research included in this review focuses upon the impact of schools and/or headteachers.

The process of compiling the report had three components:

1) A desk review of the available research literature.
2) Consultations with leading researchers in the field.
3) A meeting of the review group overseeing the research.

The report has been divided into six chapters. Chapter one comprises this introduction, chapter two comprises an overview of how the literature review has been framed, chapters three to five summarise and evaluate what the research studies have to say. In the final chapter, chapter six, the conclusions of the report are presented together with recommendations for further research.

1.1 the current context

This report has been commissioned at a significant time. A review of the research into schools with a Christian ethos has the potential to make an important contribution at a point when the role of faith in education is under much public scrutiny.

In Western liberal democratic societies, education has become a key focus for our political leaders; witness, for example, the massive investment in the US and UK in the two policies *No Child Left Behind* (One Hundred and Seventh Congress of the United States of America, 2001) and *Every Child Matters* (Treasury, 2003). Three agendas appear to dominate education policy:

1) Concern about declining standards of academic achievement and progress.
2) Concern about character education and well-being.
3) The role of faith schools in national systems of education.

1.1.1 academic achievement and progress

In the United Kingdom, recent government education policies have implemented key curriculum initiatives and assessment strategies for English, mathematics and science and extended the number of specialist schools and Academies, many of which are sponsored by faith groups. Within this policy discourse, education is viewed primarily as a means to realise equal opportunity and wealth creation in society. Part of the sub-text of these policies has been the reorientation of Western economies towards the financial and service sectors, which required a differently skilled workforce. Tomlinson (2001) writes that, in the 1980s and 1990s, decline in national education standards in the UK and US in comparison to Pacific Rim countries focussed policy makers' attention on curriculum, measures of achievement and systems of institutional accountability. This policy shift has consequences for all state-maintained schools in England and Wales, but particularly for schools with a Christian ethos. The publication of national school league tables, the introduction of a national curriculum and testing, together with parental choice, have placed English schools in a quasi-market where impact is judged by pupil performance. Nearly a third of maintained schools in England and Wales have a religious character (DCSF, 2007). These schools continue to be popular with parents and they often do very well in published national league tables. The Labour government has championed the expansion of state-funded schools with a religious character on the basis that they raise standards and attainment.

1.1.2 character education and well-being

There is also a growing interest among policy makers in the models of character formation and citizenship offered by schools with a Christian ethos in the UK, US and Australasia. Brown (2003) argues that within UK civil society and culture there has been a reaction against institutions, such as organised religion, which traditionally had a role in guarding morality and in motivating community and a civic sense of responsibility. Concern about declining standards of behaviour and the breakdown of traditional models of civic society have focussed attention on the role of schools in character formation and values development. King (2009) argues that there has also been a global awakening of interest in spirituality decoupled from traditional religious or theological understandings of the spiritual. In particular, King sets this against the increasing threat of the economic recession to the orientation of Western society towards materialism and capitalist goals.

> *For some, schools with a Christian ethos offer grounding in morality and ethics perceived to be missing from wider society.*

Given these twin preoccupations with declining standards and the breakdown of traditional economic and social models it is not difficult to explain the interest in the contribution Christian ethos schools make to national systems of education. The perception remains that Christian ethos schools achieve higher educational standards and produce pupils with a reassuring sense of values and civic responsibility. For some parents and teachers schools with a Christian ethos offer grounding in morality and ethics perceived to be missing from wider society. For many in government they offer a way of promoting the shared values of 'British-ness' which are thought to be fundamental to community cohesion and preventing violent extremism.

1.1.3 the role of faith schools

There has also been considerable interest in the contribution that schools with a Christian ethos make to social cohesion, particularly in the wake of the terrorist attacks of 9/11 and 7/7. Christian denominations have an historic role as providers of education in England, particularly among the urban poor. The Christian character of state funded schools and the influence of Christian beliefs and ethics was uncontroversial for policy makers in 1944 and 1988[1], but today the principle of state funding for faith schools is highly contested. Fears about the global rise of religious fundamentalism have reinforced perceptions that education within a particular religious tradition is socially divisive (e.g. Ouseley, 2001, Toynbee, 2006). In the UK a very effective lobby has been formed in opposition to the expansion of faith schooling. This lobby includes organisations such as the National Secular Society, the British Humanist Association and the coalition group Accord[2]. Accord is a coalition of groups campaigning for the legislative reform of religious schools. Accord opposes the expansion of state-funded religious schools operating restrictive or discriminatory practices and opposes legislation which, they argue, gives religious schools special exemption from human rights legislation. The accusation has been levied by this lobby that schools with a Christian ethos are divisive on the basis of class as well as on ethnic, racial and religious grounds. It is argued that they are able to promote high pupil performance because they are socially selective. For some, schools with a Christian ethos are an anachronism badly out of step with the real issues that face contemporary secular society in the West.

1.2 summary

Considerable amounts of money and resources are being invested by the state, the church and by parents in Christian ethos schools around the world. Schools with a Christian ethos are both attacked and defended in relation to their contribution to the standards agenda, character formation, spiritual development and nurture within the Christian faith community. It is timely that this review should consider what the research evidence tells us about the impact of such schools. The evidence needs to be explored both in relation to their purpose and goals, and in relation to the wider debate about what education can or should provide for young people in contemporary society. This report will be of interest to anyone asking the question, 'What do schools with a Christian ethos offer to pupils in the modern age?'

chapter 1 - references

1. Prior to 1944 a dual system of board and local education authority schools had developed alongside church schools. Most schools provided elementary education for pupils aged between 5 and 14. The 1944 Education Act created a partnership in the provision of schooling between church authorities and the state. In addition, religious instruction and a daily act of corporate worship were made compulsory in all schools. The 1988 Education Reform Act also required that all schools hold a daily act of collective worship, wholly or mainly Christian in character, and preserved the compulsory nature of Religious Education in the curriculum. These requirements are still current.

2. www.secularism.org.uk, www.humanism.org.uk, www.accordcoalition.org.uk.

framing the review

There is much diversity within the current research literature which focuses on the impact of schools with a Christian ethos. This diversity relates both to types of school and to the nature of the research. A wide range of methodologies, with their attendant assumptions about the nature of data, have been employed. A range of theological understandings about the nature of Christian belief and, hence, Christian distinctiveness[1] is also represented within the research. This impacts assumptions made about appropriate goals and outcomes for pupils attending these schools. It also means that a range of definitions for terms such as 'spirituality' or 'Christian ethos' have been used in the research reviewed. This report deliberately avoids imposing its own definitions of such terms, instead it highlights the way that the definitions change according to the assumptions underpinning the research. It is, therefore, important for rigour that this report attempts to make clear the criteria on which research evidence has been included in the review and the analytical framework that has been employed to handle this diversity.

2.1 criteria for selection

A database of approximately 100 items has been generated for this review. A diagram of the literature search and the criteria for selection can be found in appendix 1. There exists a significant body of literature which consists of discussion and critical reflection on what Christian ethos education might ideally comprise. This is different from the empirical research into the impact of schools with a Christian ethos and in this report it is referred to as 'discussion literature'. This discussion literature comprises both an academic and a grey literature. Academic literature has been defined as peer reviewed, or subject to an equivalent process such as a university viva and therefore of a published or publishable standard. Grey literature refers to literature which has not undergone this process, such as internal documents written for educational practitioners, talks given at in service training (INSET) settings, or to churches and for a general audience. The database contains around twenty such discussion items which have been retained and used for the purpose of providing context for the empirical studies. Including such material is important for the following three reasons:

1) It recognises that important issues have been raised and significant work done outside of mainstream academic settings because it has been difficult, particularly in the UK, for researchers in this field to get funding and to have a voice.

2) It reflects the fact that there are peer-reviewed journals such as the *Journal of Education and Christian Belief* and the *Journal of Christian Education* where discussion and critical reflection tends to predominate over empirical research studies.

3) This type of discussion and critical reflection provides a context for the empirical research and in some cases helps to explain assumptions about methodology and theological approaches to Christian belief and hence ethos and education.

Nevertheless, it remained the main objective of this review to summarise and evaluate the contribution of empirical studies to our knowledge of the impact of schools with a Christian ethos. This responds directly to Grace's call (2003a) for 'evidence-based' rather than ideological or 'prejudice-based' research (p. 149). Studies were restricted in most cases to those carried out in approximately the last ten years. This is because major reforms of education policy at national level and major reports relating to the provision of maintained church schools had been published in the UK during this time. Notably *Every child matters* (Treasury, 2003), *Faith in the system* (DCSF, 2007) and the Church of England report *The Way Ahead* (Dearing, 2001). There are one or two exceptions to this where an earlier study was considered to have been significant and continued to make a relevant contribution to the research.

In addition to limiting studies by date, an attempt was made to restrict studies to those relevant to the review's key question about the 'impact' of primary and secondary schools with a Christian ethos. From an initial literature search it became apparent that research pertaining to beliefs, attitudes, behaviours and spiritual development of pupils uses a range of different keywords; for example 'values' or 'spirituality'. The ways in which these might be variously defined is discussed below with reference to the analytical framework. In order to be as comprehensive as possible in searching the literature a list of key words that might be used as proxies was generated in consultation with ten researchers. The five proxies generated were:

1) (Christian) ethos.
2) Religious identity/affiliation/attitudes.
3) Values and character education.
4) Attainment.
5) Spirituality and spiritual health.

With dates and keyword proxies in place the following academic databases and journals were searched for peer reviewed content:

1) British Education Research Index.
2) Australian Research Index.
3) Oxford Libraries Information Service (OLIS).[2]
4) British Journal of Religious Education.
5) Journal of Beliefs and Values.
6) Journal of Education and Christian Belief.
7) Journal of Christian Education.
8) Journal of International Children's Spirituality.

In addition, studies were included that had been recommended via consultation with the researchers and by following up cited references within items. A table of the studies grouped by keyword can be found in appendix 2.

2.2 analytical framework

A diagram of the analytical framework developed for this review can be found in appendix 3 at the end of this report. The framework that has been developed is inductive, in that it has been generated from the diversity and definitions found within the literature reviewed. The strength of this approach is that it does not impose a prior methodological or theoretical framework from outside of the research. This can be seen to be important given the diversity of the field. Nor does it impose *a priori* judgements about what makes for appropriate impact in relation to Christian ethos schooling. The weakness of this approach is that it means current research foci and agendas have the potential to drive evaluation of the research and also the recommendations for future research that this report seeks to make. The review has sought to overcome this weakness via critical discussion of research paradigms and by the development of a framework for future research. The discussion and the framework are presented in chapter six.

> *It remained the main objective of this review to summarise and evaluate the contribution of empirical studies to our knowledge of the impact of schools with a Christian ethos.*

2.2.1 definitions

Whilst the report has not attempted to predefine terms such as 'spirituality' and 'ethos' the analytical framework for this review had to engage with a range of these problematic terms in relation to selecting and organising studies for review. These terms operate at three levels: i) within studies, ii) within groups of studies and iii) by school type.

The main way that the studies have been organised in this report is by school type. There is some difficulty in arriving at a definition of what counts as 'a school with a Christian ethos', particularly because ethos is already a contested term within the literature. It is necessary to reflect on these descriptive terms and to recognise that categories like 'Church of England schools' or 'Independent schools' are not homogenous. Allder (1993) writes that ethos is most commonly understood via other associated terms or concepts such as 'ambience' or 'spirit' (p. 69). These convey a sense of a pervasive mood, which in turn derives from a shared history of social interactions. McLaughlin (2005) defined ethos as 'the prevalent or characteristic tone, spirit or sentiment informing an identifiable entity involving human life and interaction' (p. 311). He further argued that "intended" ethos as well as an "experienced" ethos can be pointed to in the case of an ethos which is deliberately shaped or stipulated (p. 312). This would be the case in a school with a defined religious character. Green (forthcoming) has found that this is the most common understanding of ethos found within the literature around Christian ethos schools and demonstrated that it can be successfully used in the study of school culture where ethos is deliberately informed by a theological worldview. It should, however, be noted that not all of the studies included in the review research the impact of Christian ethos. In order to maximise the evidence collected, studies that survey pupil attitudes and performance have also been included.

> *Ethos is most commonly understood via other associated terms or concepts such as 'ambience' or 'spirit'.*

A list of school type descriptors was generated from the studies in the database. The descriptors found within the English and Welsh literature comprise:

1) Maintained church schools including Church of England Voluntary Aided (VA) and Controlled (VC) and Catholic VA schools.[3]

2) Traditional independent schools with a Christian foundation, for example schools affiliated with the Bloxham Project (see chapter 4, section 2 for a description of the project) or with The Independent Schools Christian Alliance (TISCA).

3) The new Christian schools (see chapter 4, section 2 for a description of these schools). This includes those affiliated to The Christian Schools Trust (CST), Christian Education Europe (CEE) and Accelerated Christian Education schools (ACE).

4) CTCs and Academies sponsored by Christian foundations.

The list of descriptors found within the international literature comprises:

1) Maintained church schools – this means totally within government control and may refer to either the Anglican or the Roman Catholic Church depending on the country.

2) Wholly independent schools with a Christian foundation and independent Christian schools which are subsidised by the state.[4]

This review recognises that each of these types themselves comprise considerable diversity of schools. The descriptors have therefore been applied within the framework with the caveat that the type of institution being researched will be described for each study reviewed.

2.2.2 methodologies and proxies for researching impact

Three broad methodological approaches dominate the studies reviewed: (i) ethnographic and/or case study design, (ii) survey design using questionnaires (sometimes also supplemented with interviews) and (iii) statistical reviews either of survey data or of examination and achievement data sets. Not surprisingly, these reflect the key methodological approaches in education and social science research. It also became apparent from this survey that clear patterns could be identified in relation to the *focus* of the research i.e. whether beliefs, attitudes, behaviour or spiritual development. There follows a brief summary of the key foci together with the methodologies and proxy terms commonly used by the studies:

1) Studies based on ethnographic or on case study design primarily investigated the impact of Christian ethos in relation to belief, with an emphasis on how beliefs were impacted by institutional structures. The proxy terms encountered most often here were ethos, values and character.

2) Another set of studies utilising questionnaire or survey design focussed on spiritual development. In these studies the concept of spirituality was often decoupled from traditional definitions of the spiritual associated with institutional religion. The impact of Christian ethos tended to be a secondary theme in these studies since they were more concerned to deconstruct traditional models of spirituality. The most common proxy for these studies was 'spirituality' and to a much lesser degree 'identity'.

3) A considerable number of the studies into the impact of Christian ethos schools on attitudes use survey design, stemming from the empirical tradition within the social sciences and social psychology. This approach has the advantage of being able to generate large enough data sets from which statistical significance may be demonstrated. Conclusions from this research are capable of generalisation to a wider population. The proxies encountered most often within these studies were religious identity, religious affiliation, religious attitudes and values.

> *The report attempts to map the contribution that empirical research makes to what we know about the impact of schools with a Christian ethos upon belief, attitudes, behaviours and spiritual development.*

4) The final methodological approach also utilised large data sets and statistical techniques, but focussed on the official data collected by government, relating to pupil attainment and school performance. The focus of these studies is the impact that schools with a Christian ethos have upon performance, or behaviour (when understood as pupil/cohort characteristics). Many of these studies are influenced by the School Effectiveness School Improvement (SESI) research paradigm. This assumes that efficient school structures and highly accountable leadership and processes can maximise productivity and output (see for example Teddlie and Reynolds, 2000). The proxy used most often in the literature with this type of focus was attainment.

2.2.3 summary

In summary, the analytical framework allows for diversity in school type and in methodological approaches and terminology. Studies are grouped in such a way that summary and evaluation can take account of evidence from individual pieces of research and assess it within the study's own frame of reference. Comparisons and wider conclusions may also be drawn where appropriate. In this way the report attempts to map the contribution that empirical research makes to what we know about the impact of schools with a Christian ethos upon belief, attitudes, behaviours and spiritual development. Furthermore the framework allows for critical reflection upon the assumptions that currently frame the way Christian distinctiveness is conceptualised and researched.

chapter 2 - references

1. The phrase 'distinctively Christian' has come to prominence through its use in the influential report *The Way Ahead* published by the Church of England (Dearing, 2001).

2. OLIS is a database of the Bodleian Library's collection; this is a copyright library.

3. In VA schools the governing body employs the staff, the school sets its own admission arrangements, and buildings and land are owned by a charitable foundation; in VC schools, local education authorities remain in control of staffing and admissions.

4. For an excellent overview of the different policies regarding the funding of Christian schools in Europe and Australasia see Glenn, C. & De Groof, J. (2002) *Finding the right balance: freedom, autonomy and accountability in education* (Urtgeverij, Netherlands: Lemma, 2002).

maintained church schools in England and Wales

The biggest providers of Christian ethos voluntary schools in England are the Catholic Church and the Church of England. The review found that this dominance was also reflected in the focus of the research. In addition, the review includes a limited number of studies relating to maintained schools supported by other Christian denominations in England and Wales.

3.1 Catholic schools

Seminal work carried out by Bryk *et al.* (1993) into Catholic schools in the US (see chapter 5 section 3) has somewhat raised the bar for research into Catholic schooling. There is nothing in England and Wales on the scale of this ten year US project and Bryk's *Catholic schools and the common good* has been influential the UK. Bryk *et al.* concluded that Catholic schools in America offered a distinctive form of education capable of promoting a humane social order, or the common good. They argued that this distinctiveness rested upon the tradition of Catholic schooling together with the mutual reinforcement of Catholic identity through the community of school, church and family. The review found that this concept of a distinctive Catholic education and of the impact of the Catholic school effect hovered in the background of many of the research studies consulted.

3.1.1 Catholic primary schools

With the exception of a review of attainment in Catholic education at both primary and secondary levels, the literature review did not find any studies conducted in the last ten years that relate to Catholic primary schools either in the maintained or in the private sector. Morris and Godfrey (2006) reviewed the performance of Catholic primary schools using the Department for Education and Science (DfES) value added scores for 2004. They concluded that pupils attending Catholic primary schools have a higher than average mean points score on national tests for English, mathematics and science. This evidence is discussed in more depth below in relation to the secondary school findings, but would appear to lend support to the widespread perception that Catholic school pupils perform better on government measures of attainment.

3.1.2 Catholic secondary schools

A search for empirical research carried out into maintained Catholic secondary schools yielded more results. The focus of these studies fell broadly into 2 categories: i) the impact of Catholic school ethos on pupils' attitudes, attainment and spirituality, and ii) research into the nature of Catholic education and mission. Despite the different methodologies employed within this research a desire to explain and account for Catholic school effect underscores them all. This suggests that Bryk *et al's* (1993) research has been influential. It is necessary to be aware that some researchers are a little cautious about exporting Bryk *et al's* findings as assumptions for a UK context. It is also necessary to point out that these studies in no way reflect the diversity of individual Catholic secondary schools and the different impact at an institutional level which they may have upon pupils.

Francis has conducted research into the impact of Catholic schools upon pupil attitudes. Curran and Francis (1996) developed a scale which measures Catholic identity and which was employed among 11 to 12 year olds attending Catholic secondary schools. Francis (Francis & Robbins, 2005) writes that the responses to this survey 'indicated a basically positive view of being Catholic' (p. 116). The research found that Catholic background, Catholic home, church involvement and attending a Catholic secondary school were all important in the promotion of Catholic identity and a positive attitude towards being Catholic.

Francis' (2002) analysis of 13-15 year olds attending Catholic secondary schools drew on a database of approximately 13,000 teenagers whose values were profiled for the 'Religion and Values Today Project' (Francis, 2001).[1] In the study Francis draws attention to four distinct groups, or 'communities of values' as he describes them, which can be identified amongst the pupils: i) active Catholics, ii) sliding Catholics, iii) lapsed Catholics, and iv) non-Catholics (2002, p. 75). This provides more information about the relationship between religious commitment and attitudes reported by Catholic school pupils. When the moral values of pupils attending Catholic school were compared with those attending non-denominational schools the research found that practising Catholic pupils at Catholic schools recorded higher scores. This supports Gill's (1999) argument that committed churchgoing is a significant predictor of religious attitudes in its own right. Lapsed Catholic pupils recorded lower scores than pupils in non-denominational schools. With regard to religious values, practising Catholics again recorded higher scores than pupils in non-denominational schools. The scores for lapsed Catholics were nearly the same as those for pupils in non-denominational schools. Thus, Francis argues that lapsed Catholics presented a greater threat to the communities of higher moral and religious values in Catholic secondary schools than non-Catholic pupils. Whilst the religion and values database does not report on individual school effect, it does support the wider argument that there is a relationship between active church commitment and Catholic secondary education which reinforces positive attitudes towards moral and religious values held within those communities.

Francis argues that this type of empirical evidence suggests that attending a Catholic school is likely to predict individual differences across a wider range of areas and he has examined it in relation to the measure of spiritual health developed by Fisher (1999). Spiritual health is not a straightforward proxy within the literature for the impact of schools with a Christian ethos on spiritual development. Whilst Fisher's instrument can measure the reported levels of spiritual health of pupils, it does not account for the impact that the school ethos may have had on spiritual health. Nevertheless Fisher's notion of spiritual health, and the way Francis has developed it, constitutes one of the few research approaches found in the literature that directly relates to concepts of spirituality. Fisher's model for spiritual health posits that there are four domains of spiritual well-being: i) personal, ii) communal, iii) environmental, and iv) transcendental (Fisher *et al.*, 2000). Fisher argues that qualitative research into spirituality and child development is costly, time consuming and potentially open to researcher bias (for qualitative research perspectives on this see Hay and Nye, 2006, Erricker, 2007). Fisher thus used survey data to construct a measure that would be quick and convenient to administer to large numbers of respondents. He has developed spiritual health measures for use with secondary school pupils and with pre-adolescents. These measures investigate the quality of the relationships people have with themselves, others, the environment and God (or the transcendent) (Fisher, 2004, p. 308).

> *There is a relationship between active church commitment and Catholic secondary education which reinforces positive attitudes towards moral and religious values.*

Francis & Robbins (2005) used these four domains to examine the relationship between attending denominational schools and spiritual health. Francis drew on data from 23,418 young people living in urban areas. This data was part of a larger database comprising over 30,000 adolescents surveyed using a revised version of the Centymca Attitude Inventory. Francis compared the results of pupils educated in maintained Catholic secondary schools with those educated in non-denominational state-maintained secondary schools. All of these schools were in urban areas. Overall, although the pupils at both types of schools shared a number of indicators of spiritual health, there were also statistically significant differences between the two groups in respect to all four domains of spiritual health. In the personal domain Catholic pupils enjoyed more sense of purpose of life, but in the communal domain, they demonstrated greater anxiety about relationships and bullying. In the environmental domain, Catholic pupils showed a greater concern for world development, and in the transcendental domain, demonstrated a greater commitment to traditional religion, but they were also more supportive of non-traditional religion such as believing in horoscopes. Francis argues that Catholic secondary schools bring to the 'urban environment communities in which belief in God is the norm' (p. 122). Catholic education has a traditional mission to nurture faith and to provide for its poor (Grace, 2003b). In the light of this, Francis & Robbins'(2005) research does indicate that Catholic schools may influence beliefs about the transcendent and bring a greater sense of purpose to urban environments where there are likely to be higher levels of socio-economic deprivation. Set against this, however, is the lack of information about individual schools and data that might enable us to put these findings in a local urban context. Furthermore, the data suggests that there is considerable variation within the domains, and that on several indicators, there is no discernible difference between pupils attending Catholic schools and non-denominational schools. The data also seemed to suggest that Catholic school pupils from urban environments are more worried about bullying, but the spiritual health measure cannot explain whether this is caused by factors associated with urban community living or school effect. This evidence does not offer a comprehensive picture of the impact that schools with a Catholic ethos have on spiritual development.

Pupils who were more socially disadvantaged, on average, did better in Catholic secondary schools compared to their counterparts attending non-Catholic secondary schools.

Statistical research, conducted on official data collected by the government, accounts for eight studies in the database (relating to Catholic schools). This research broadly provides empirical evidence to support the widespread public perception that maintained Catholic secondary schools do better, in terms of attainment and pupil progress, than non-denominational schools. The exception to this is the post-16 sector, where Morris (2007) found considerable variation in pupil achievement in relation to the size and status of Catholic sixth forms. Morris found that when the results from pupils attending different types of Catholic sixth form are aggregated, pupils appear to be under-performing compared to pupils at non-Catholic sixth forms. Since this was the only Catholic post-16 study included in the review the rest of this discussion should be taken as referring to Key Stages 3 and 4 (11-16).

Using the DfES valued added scores as a measure of pupil progress, Morris and Godfrey (2006) found that secondary school pupils in the Catholic maintained sector were performing, on average, better than those attending non-Catholic schools at Key Stages 3 and 4. This remained the case when adjustments were made for factors known to affect levels of achievement, such as prior attainment or socio-economic status (SES). The criticism most commonly levelled at the maintained Catholic school sector in relation to attainment is that they select pupils with a social class, cultural and economic advantage (Pennell *et al.* 2007). These findings are therefore significant because the higher attainment and progress of Catholic school pupils evident in the research could not be explained by socio-economic factors or pupil characteristics. Indeed Morris (2005) found that pupils who were more socially disadvantaged, on average, did better in Catholic secondary schools compared to their counterparts attending non-Catholic secondary schools. Morris and Godfrey (2006) acknowledge that their findings do not definitively demonstrate the existence of a 'Catholic school effect' because the results only relate to the 2004 cohort of pupils. They also warn against the temptation to conflate the primary mission and goal of Catholic education with attainment and academic excellence (p. 32). The implication of this is that although the government may make higher attainment and progress the sole basis on which it supports faith schools, academic excellence should not be the basis on which the leadership of the Catholic Church defends them. This raises important wider questions about the motivation and agenda for research into the impact of Christian ethos schools and the report will return to this issue in chapter six.

Another argument commonly used to explain higher performance at GCSE[2] amongst Catholic school pupils is that because GCSE Religious Education (RE) is a compulsory subject, pupils sit more examinations in the first place, thereby artificially inflating their GCSE point scores. Research by Godfrey and Morris (2008) appears to successfully refute this for all types of faith school pupils as well as Catholic school pupils. Although their study does confirm that pupils at Catholic and other types of faith schools are more likely to sit GCSE RE, the most significant feature of their analysis is that, 'pupils in all types of faith school score higher *without* the contribution of points gained in Religious Education examinations than pupils in non-faith schools score *with* their Religious Education points' (p. 221). Similarly Morris' (1998a, 1998b, 2005, 2007) analysis of OfSTED[3] inspection reports for Catholic secondary schools challenges the argument commonly made that strong leadership and better quality teaching and learning explain effective schooling and therefore the higher attainment and progress of pupils in Catholic schools. Morris found that, 'overall Catholic schools' effectiveness in achieving higher general standards has less to do with the quality of teaching than with their functioning as a community and the effects it exerts on pupils' personal development and behaviour' (p. 186). Using OfSTED measures in research is problematic for a number of reasons. Not only have OfSTED definitions of effectiveness and performance been highly contested since their inception, but the measures have developed and thus have changed considerably over time, making longitudinal comparison very difficult. There may also be variance in how individual OfSTED inspection teams apply in practice the centrally determined criteria. Morris thus acknowledges that the significance of his results may only be speculative and that the data can only be indicative of causes.

In his study of the impact of changing education policy on the traditional conceptions of Catholic education in the UK, Grace (2002) has attempted to analyse Catholic school effect in terms of Catholicity. Catholicity refers to the spiritual and religious sense of pupils expressed in particular forms within Catholic tradition. The Catholicity of pupils would be measured in terms of their attendance at Mass, their understanding of Catholic doctrine and the number of religious vocations among school leavers. This qualitative research primarily surveyed the challenges facing the leaders of Catholic secondary schools in urban areas. Grace concluded that Catholic school leaders were able to draw upon spiritual capital stemming from their religious identity and heritage in the face of secular challenges to traditional concepts of mission and morality in Catholic faith-based education. The study also included data compiled from focus group discussions involving fifty Year Ten pupils from five inner London Catholic secondary schools. Ten pupils from each school were selected by the schools; five were selected who were regarded as examples of 'model pupils' and who would strongly identify with school, and five were selected that were regarded as 'troublesome school resistors' (p. 231). These two groups of pupils are referred to informally within Grace's discussion as 'saints' and 'sinners' (p. 231). The Year Ten pupils 'were asked to reflect upon the extent to which the principles' in their school mission statements 'had been realised in their own experience of Catholic schooling' (p. 231). Six themes comprising i) the dignity of the person, ii) forgiveness and justice, iii) racism, iv) bullying, v) quality of teaching, and vi) Catholicity emerged from the focus-group discussions.

> *Although the government may make higher attainment and progress the sole basis on which it supports faith schools, academic excellence should not be the basis on which the leadership of the Catholic Church defends them.*

The research found that 'dignity of the person' was mentioned in most of the school mission statements and that the majority of pupils endorsed it as a reality in their experience. The saints and the sinners disagreed much more over the presence of justice and forgiveness in their school experience with the sinners more likely to reflect on encounters with injustice or lack of forgiveness. In only two cases was reference made to the presence of racism and in only one school was any reference made to bullying. Most pupils commented on positive experience of multi-ethnic and cultural harmony. The pupils appeared to regard the quality of teaching as an outworking of respect for the dignity of the person. Only in one school, which had a large turnover of supply teachers, were negative comments made about the quality of teaching. Finally, with regard to Catholicity, Grace writes that, 'in general the pupils spoke positively of their experience of Catholic religious teaching and liturgy in the schools' (p. 233). This is a very small project in which the voices of pupils have been considered in relation to the impact of mission integrity in Catholic schools. Whilst it offers an example of how qualitative research might explore the impact of Catholic ethos on beliefs, attitudes, behaviours and spiritual development, no generally applicable conclusions may be drawn from the data.

3.1.3 summary

To summarise, the research on Roman Catholic schools in the UK does appear to be influenced by Bryk *et al's* highly significant study of the nature, setting and impact of Catholic schooling in the US. His arguments about the importance of coherent mission and the significance of the church, school and community structures in reinforcing Catholic ethos, morality and values, frame the assumptions about the reality of school effect in many of these studies. The research is mainly grouped around two foci: i) research into attitudes and ii) into attainment. The work done by Francis and Robbins (2005) on religious attitudes and spiritual health supports the conclusion that pupils attending Catholic secondary schools display a distinctive values profile. This work also demonstrates that active participation in the Catholic Church and faith community acts as a predictor of individual difference. This lends weight to the argument that Catholic school effect may well be linked to such factors as the relationship between church, community and school. Similarly the research into the achievement and progress of pupils at Catholic primary and secondary schools demonstrates that the higher scores cannot be explained away by prior attainment and SES, or by sitting RE as an additional GCSE subject. Morris' survey of OfSTED data (1998a) also casts doubt on SESI explanations that attribute school effectiveness to particular leadership styles and to a superior quality of teaching and learning. These researchers are convinced that school effect explains the difference in attainment and progress at Catholic schools. Neither the research into attitudes nor into attainment, however, really demonstrates what causes this Catholic school effect. Attempts to describe what it might consist of can only be speculative, because these studies have aggregated responses and achievement data from across different schools. The approach tentatively offered within Grace's research (2002) might be a way forward in this respect. The review did not, however, find any other recent examples of ethnographic or qualitative research into the impact of Catholic schools upon beliefs, attitude, behaviour and spiritual development in maintained Catholic schools.

> *These researchers are convinced that school effect explains the difference in attainment and progress at Catholic schools.*

3.2 Church of England schools

The Church of England published *The Way Ahead* report (Dearing, 2001) in 2001. It was intended to have a significant impact upon the way in which Church of England schools understood their educational mission in terms of Christian distinctiveness. The report argued that church schools stand at 'the centre of the church's mission to the nation' (p. 10). *The Way Ahead* made four main recommendations:

1) More resources should be made available for education.
2) Church of England schools should become voluntary aided rather than controlled. This preserves control over such factors as governance, staffing and the Religious Education curriculum.
3) The number of Church of England secondary schools should be expanded with a target of 100 new schools by 2010.
4) A commission into church schools and colleges should be established.

The review revealed a common thread in the subsequent research. This concerned the extent to which *The Way Ahead* report has impacted practice, particularly in the areas of transmitting values and shaping a distinctively Christian ethos in Church of England schools. In some of the research, therefore, the focus is on the relationship between policy and school rather than the school's impact on pupil beliefs, attitudes, behaviour and spiritual development.

3.2.1 Church of England primary schools

As with the research into the maintained Catholic sector, the balance of studies is weighted heavily in favour of Church of England secondary schools. The review did, however, find examples of research carried out in relation to Church of England and Church of Wales primary schools. Arthur and Godfrey (2005) demonstrate that at Key Stage Two, pupils at Church of England primary schools attained, on average, a higher point score and made greater progress when compared to pupils at non-faith schools. When compared to pupils at Catholic primary schools, however, pupils at Church of England schools had a slightly lower score. When value added scores were adjusted for individual pupil characteristics the differences between Church of England pupils' and Catholic pupils' scores were halved. Accounting for school characteristics also reduced the gap between Church of England and non-faith school pupils. As Arthur and Godfrey explain, this implies that the attainment of pupils in Church of England over pupils in non-faith schools is 'largely but not entirely attributable to the prior attainment and other characteristics of the pupils recruited' (p. 18). In other words this research does not support to the same extent it did for Catholic primary schools the argument that school effect explains the higher attainment and better progress of Church of England primary school pupils. The caveat must be made, however, that this is evidence relating to a single cohort of pupils and that it aggregates results; it does not report on an individual school basis.

Jelfs (2008) researched the Christian distinctiveness of Church of England primary schools. Christian distinctiveness was explored in relation to current educational discourse and changing perspectives of religion in the light of post-modern ways of knowing and experiencing the world. Jelfs' research consisted of two phases of data collection. In the first phase she surveyed all the Church of England schools in one diocese using the 'Effective Lifelong Learning Inventory' (ELLI) questionnaire.[4] The second phase comprised ethnographic case-studies of three Church of England primary schools and one joint Church of England/Catholic primary school in the same diocese. This was a purposive sample; one school was voluntary controlled and the other three were voluntary aided. Ethnographic data was collected through participant observation, interviews and focus groups with parents and pupils. Jelfs' findings indicated that the Church of England schools were committed to their religious Christian foundation. This was demonstrated by their links to the church, the religious dimension within the life of the school and in the value placed on caring relationships, academic achievement and personal development. But Jelfs also found that the schools had not attempted to critique the dominant educational discourse within which they operated and they had not developed a 'significantly distinctive approach' (p. 2). Jelfs argues that the Christian character of Church of England schools is thus compromised by 'an unwitting compliance with values and principles that may compromise those they seek to promote' (p. 2). Jelfs also argues that this exposes a failure to engage with the Christian faith as a coherent rationale for life and learning. Jelfs proposes a model which re-engages concepts of knowing and learning with relational epistemology. She argues that this challenges an older 'belief-centred' paradigm of Christian faith that emphasised authority, moralism and belief in central doctrines (p. 65). The new paradigm she offers embraces post-modern ways of knowing by emphasising the relational aspects of living as a Christian. Jelfs argues that understanding the Christian faith as a way of 'seeing, knowing and doing' offers a theological perspective to the task of distinctive Christian education (p. 80).

> *Understanding the Christian faith as a way of 'seeing, knowing and doing' offers a theological perspective to the task of distinctive Christian education.*

Three further studies researched the perspectives of church primary school headteachers. One study was based in England, two in Wales. These research studies do not primarily explore the impact that church primary schools may have on the beliefs, attitudes, behaviours and spiritual development of pupils. Nevertheless, providing evidence of the ways in which headteachers envisage the role of the school in spiritual development and in the teaching of RE does begin to build an impression of what might be shaping pupils' experience in practice.

Johnson and McCreery (1999) were particularly interested in the Church of England's historic twin mission to provide education for the poor and nurture in the Anglican faith. They asked how this mission was perceived by headteachers in relation to contemporary multi-faith society. They argue that education reform has fundamentally changed the nature of the role of headteachers because they are accountable to multiple and varied audiences comprised of governors, parents and inspectors (including diocesan board inspectors). Their hypothesis was that these audiences may influence the ways in which spirituality is viewed in schools. They interviewed the headteachers of seven primary schools, which were all in one London diocese. Two of the schools were voluntary controlled and five voluntary aided, all of them set their own admissions policies because they were over-subscribed. Although there was considerable variation in admission policies, all of the schools gave Anglican pupils priority. The study found that parental expectations in relation to discipline and character were a significant influence on headteachers. The headteachers reported that parents chose Church of England schools because they associated them with good discipline and moral education. Out of the seven headteachers, five were Anglican with varying degrees of commitment. Johnson and McCreery report that there seemed to be no automatic expectation amongst the headteachers that the head of a Church of England school should be an Anglican. With regard to spirituality the research found that the headteachers tended to emphasise Christianity as a liberal value system working out in respect for others and tolerant behaviour. A number of the headteachers spoke about not wanting to be 'narrowly Anglican' but rather to share broad Christian values and to emphasise tradition over religion (p. 171). The research found that headteachers saw themselves as role models for promoting the spiritual in school, many also identified the importance of RE as a space within the curriculum for spiritual development. Collective worship was understood by all the headteachers to play a significant part in the spiritual life of the school. What emerges from this research is how elusive the term 'spiritual' was for the headteachers. Johnson and McCreery concluded that headteachers were very influenced by the pressure not to appear intolerant or narrow in their conceptions of the spiritual. They suggest that these pressures were more influential than any prior notions of Christian distinctiveness and spirituality offered by the

> *Parents chose Church of England schools because they associated them with good discipline and moral education.*

Church of England and modelled in the mission of the school. This research was carried out before *The Way Ahead* report (Dearing, 2001) was published; it would be interesting to revisit these schools to see whether concepts of spirituality had changed at all.

Davies (2007) administered a questionnaire to assess the views on spiritual development found among Church of Wales primary school headteachers. He found that although spiritual development is ostensibly an ambiguous term, headteachers had clear views about what it meant. These views strongly correlated with their own religiosity. Most headteachers emphasised the need for pupils to be active in their own spiritual search, but were divided over whether or not spiritual development necessitated the promotion of Christian beliefs. Half of the sample believed that spirituality should not be divorced from religious tradition and these represented the headteachers who also demonstrated the highest active religious commitment in their personal lives. Accordingly, headteachers with the lowest levels of active religious commitment did not believe that Christian belief should be promoted in school and felt that the promotion of spiritual development should be divorced from all forms of religious tradition. A tenth of headteachers felt that school had no legitimate role at all in promoting spiritual development and that this should be left to the home.

Davies and Francis (2007) used data provided by church primary school headteachers in Wales to survey the approaches taken towards Religious Education in school. They distinguish between three main approaches:

1) Spiritual development, in which the aim is to use pupils' own experiences to promote spiritual awareness and development.
2) World religions, which aims to teach pupils about the different world faiths; sometimes this is referred to as the phenomenological or multi-faith approach.
3) Christian nurture, the purpose of which is to nurture pupils in the Christian faith; this is often referred to as the confessional approach.

Francis and Davies hypothesised that the personal beliefs and religiosity among teachers would be a powerful predictor of the emphasis placed on different approaches; their analysis confirmed this finding. For example, churchgoing teachers gave more emphasis to the spiritual dimension of Religious Education compared with teachers who did not attend church. When the individual characteristics of teachers were taken into account the research found no differences in emphasis between non-denominational schools and voluntary controlled Church primary schools in Wales. This reflects the fact that non-denominational and controlled schools both follow the locally agreed RE syllabus adopted or produced by their LEA. They found, however, that greater emphasis was placed on the spiritual development approach rather than the Christian nurture approach in voluntary aided primary schools belonging to the Church of Wales.

In summary, the research into the impact of Church of England primary schools on the higher attainment of pupils does not demonstrate that it is entirely due to school effect. Other studies in the context of Wales support the argument that religiosity and active church commitment are powerful predictors of teachers' attitudes towards religion and what might be termed more traditional conceptions of spirituality. They also demonstrate that voluntary aided schools retain more control over approaches to teaching Religious Education. This lends support to the view that aided schools are in a better position to preserve a distinctive Church ethos. Although it is not possible to generalise from qualitative research, evidence from the Johnson and McCreery (1999) study suggested that the concept of spirituality might not be well understood by Church of England school headteachers. Evidence from Jelfs' research suggests that Christian distinctiveness is not well understood in Church of England primary schools. These two studies lend weight to Jelfs' broader argument that Church schools lack an epistemology of knowing and learning capable of critiquing current educational discourse or of facilitating a coherent Christian rationale for education.

3.2.2 Church of England secondary schools

The research into Church of England secondary schools can be grouped broadly, by methodology and research focus, into two categories: i) research into religious identity, attitudes or spiritual health and ii) research into attainment. There are also a number of individual qualitative studies which research i) character and values formation, ii) the perspectives of headteachers on spiritual development, iii) the impact of *The Way Ahead* report upon headteachers and iv) the perspectives of pupils on collective worship. Clearly this represents broad diversity within a limited number of studies. Where possible studies have been grouped to enable the partial composition of a broader picture and to enable discussion around similar methodologies and research focus (see section 2.2.3). Although research into Church of England secondary schools constitutes one of the largest number of studies within the review database it is important to emphasise that they do not necessarily interact to present an argument about the impact of Church of England secondary schools as a whole.

Within his broader study of the relationship between denominational schooling and pupil attitudes, Francis has carried out extensive research into the religious affiliation and attitude of pupils at Church of England secondary schools. Although the earlier research predates *The Way Ahead* report (Dearing, 2001), examples have nevertheless been included to provide both a context for the current research and because the instruments used in the surveys do allow for broad comparisons to be made over time. Francis and Jewell (1992) compared the attitudes toward religion of Year Ten pupils attending five secondary schools in one town. Four were non-denominational secondary schools and one was a Church of England voluntary secondary school. The Church of England school had a higher proportion of pupils from churchgoing homes than the other four schools and the pupils from these homes tended to have higher SES. Within their analysis Francis and Jewell controlled for gender, social class and parental religiosity. Path analysis found that the Church of England school had exerted neither a positive nor a negative influence on pupils' religious practice, beliefs and attitudes. It should be noted that these results can only really be generalised to the location in question.

Lankshear (2005) analysed the influence of Church of England aided secondary schools on values as part of the 'Religion and Values' project (2001, see footnote 7). He reports on three areas of the values profiled: i) personal dissatisfaction, ii) moral values and iii) religious values. Three subsets of pupils attending Church of England and non-denominational schools were separately analysed: i) non-affiliates (self-identified as belonging to no religious group), ii) Anglicans and iii) Other Christians. Lankshear writes that, 'the relationship between school type and values was less clear cut than the relationship between sex and values' (p. 62). Females recorded a higher level of religious values in all three groups and more conservative moral values in the non-affiliate and Anglican groups. With respect to school type non-affiliates and Anglicans who attended Church of England aided schools recorded significantly higher levels of personal dissatisfaction compared to pupils at non-denominational schools. Pupils belonging to the Other Christians group demonstrated no significant difference in their personal dissatisfaction whether attending a Church of England or a non-denominational school. There were also no significant differences in moral values between Anglicans or Other Christians attending Church of England or non-denominational schools. The analysis did find a difference, however, between non-affiliate pupils attending the Church of England school and non-denominational schools. Non-affiliate pupils at Church of England schools displayed a more liberal set of values. Finally there were no significant differences between non-affiliates and Other Christians with respect to religious values based on school type. The study did find, however, that Anglicans attending Church of England aided schools displayed 'a significantly more positive view of religion' (p. 63). Lankshear points out that only 41.3% of pupils attending Church of England schools identify themselves as Anglican and that it cannot be assumed that this proportion of pupils is represented by the sample in his study. He also notes that without a 'school-by-school' analysis of admissions and pupil intake no conclusions can be drawn about the ways schools in his sample might vary in relation to SES and pupil characteristics (p. 65). With the proviso that there are some

These studies do not present a particularly positive impression of the impact that Church of England secondary schools have upon the attitudes of their pupils towards religion.

problems in generalising more widely from these two analyses, the Francis and Jewell (1992) and Lankshear (2005) studies do not present a particularly positive impression of the impact that Church of England secondary schools have upon the attitudes of their pupils towards religion.

This impression is confirmed by a selective comparison of six LEA schools and five Church of England schools carried out in Birmingham by Arthur (2009). Almost half of the white population in the area where the research was carried out said that they were members of the Church of England. Analysis based on two similar questionnaires shows that a third of the students in the Anglican schools claimed to be members of the Church of England but Arthur concludes that 'there was little evidence in terms of practice or belief that the majority held any specifically Christian beliefs' (p. 2). One of the most significant findings of this comparison is that questionnaire responses given by 'Other Christian' (Catholic and Evangelical) pupils and Muslim pupils were very similar. Responses given by Church of England pupils were very similar to those pupils who claimed to be 'non religious'. Arthur writes that Muslim pupils 'are more positive and sometimes far more positive about: religion, about their neighbours, and being taught character at home – than Anglicans and the non-religious groups, although Catholics and evangelicals in the C of E schools match this Muslim positivity' (p.2).

> **Pupils attending Church of England schools shared indicators of spiritual health in common with pupils in non-denominational schools.**

Francis & Robbins (2005) analysed the relationship between attending Church of England schools in an urban environment and spiritual health. As with the analysis of Catholic school pupils, Francis found that pupils attending Church of England schools shared indicators of spiritual health in common with pupils in non-denominational schools across all four domains. In the personal and communal domains pupils at Church of England secondary schools recorded signs of lower spiritual health. They were less likely to find life worth living and they were less confident in their relationships with others. For example, 64% of pupils attending Church of England schools found life really worth living compared to 69% attending non-denominational schools. Fifty-four per cent of pupils attending Church of England schools said they were worried about getting on with other people compared with 49% in non-denominational schools (p. 108-109). In the environmental and transcendental domains pupils attending Church of England schools recorded signs of better spiritual health. Church of England pupils were more likely to be concerned about world poverty and more likely to believe in God. Francis believes that the lower signs of spiritual health recorded in the personal and communal domains suggest that Church of England schools are more likely to be working with less advantaged pupils in the urban environment. He therefore concludes that in this respect,

Church of England schools are adding value to pupils' spiritual health and bringing hope to the urban environment. It is difficult to test this interpretation without more details about individual school admissions and their impact on the composition of their intake.

Arthur and Godfrey's (2005) statistical analysis of the performance of the 2004 cohort does much to empirically support the claim that pupils in maintained church schools achieve more highly and demonstrate more progress than pupils at non-denominational schools. Their analysis uses both raw scores and value added scores which are the instruments used by the government to measure pupil performance. They suggest that a review of attainment is important for public debate because it is the basis on which the government supports faith schools. This raises the question as to whether Church of England schools produce better results or are simply better at attracting pupils already predisposed to achieve highly. Arthur and Godfrey's survey does demonstrate that a large part of the difference between Anglican and non-faith schools can be accounted for by prior attainment. They are anxious to stress, however, that this does not account for all of the difference and that the residual is still noticeable. They point to research carried out by Schagen *et al.* (2002a) and by Schagen and Schagen (2005) which confirms their claim about the size of the difference. Schagen *et al.* (2002b) did, however, suggest that the higher point score at Key Stage Four could be partly attributed to the numbers of pupils taking RE as an additional GCSE at Church of England secondary schools. Godfrey and Morris (2008) have since fairly comprehensively demonstrated that this is not the case (see section 3.1.2 for the review of their findings). Arthur and Godfrey's (2005) findings only paint a national picture; they acknowledge that they are not a basis on which conclusions can be drawn about individual schools. They do demonstrate that pupils in voluntary aided schools, on average, make more academic progress than pupils in voluntary controlled schools. Arthur and Godfrey suggest that this finding may provide support for the widely held view that aided schools are more distinctive in their Church of England ethos. It was on the basis of this view that Dearing (2001) recommended in *The Way Ahead* report that, wherever possible, Church of England schools should have aided status. Arthur and Godfrey (2005) speculate that there might be a link between this distinctive ethos and attainment.

The number of qualitative studies, particularly those focussed on the impact of Church of England secondary schools upon pupils' beliefs, attitudes, behaviour and spiritual development is limited. The summaries will begin with a study that focuses on pupils before considering those that report on headteachers' perspectives.

Deakin Crick (2002) writes that, despite the challenge given to Church schools in *The Way Ahead* report, there is little research undertaken that identifies how and in what way Church schools might be distinctive. Deakin Crick's (2002) empirical case study of a voluntary aided Church of England school is an attempt to explore these questions. The research first identified the core spiritual and moral values that the school community of parents, teachers and pupils held to be of 'ultimate concern' (p. 1). The next phase of the research centred on devising a way to implement these core values to inform ethical and spiritual literacy across the curriculum. In surveying the existing practice and understanding of ethos and distinctiveness, Deakin Crick (2002) found that a 'diverse set of teaching and learning world views' was represented by the teaching staff (p. 37). She also found that although the Christian foundation of the school was perceived as having historical importance and therefore influence on ethos and values it was not considered of particular relevance to the content of what was taught. The initial survey also found that teachers and pupils lacked a common language in which to talk about values. This does not mean that they did not have clear ideas about what was important to them. Deakin Crick argues that this lack of vocabulary and the silence of the curriculum is a significant barrier to the development of distinctive whole-school approaches to ethos and values.

Deakin Crick's theory is borne out in a study of the development of values and character formation in the sixth forms of three schools, one of which was a church school, conducted by Arthur and Deakin Crick et al. (2006). This study confirms that the curriculum lacked the space for discussion of these issues and a language for discussing values. This is particularly significant, bearing in mind that the study also found that the relationships of teachers with pupils and their ability to communicate values and virtues through teaching were significant areas in which school pedagogy had the potential to influence pupil character development. In her case study Deakin Crick (2002) employed an instrument called a repertory grid[5], which has been developed as a tool to facilitate evidence about what pupils actually value. Deakin Crick argues that there is a very real danger that evidence from questionnaires only reflects what pupils feel they ought to value. The second phase of the research was based on the assumption that the gap between values espoused and actual behaviour facilitated a context in which a development of values could take place. Interventions in the curriculum were designed collaboratively with teachers, administered, and then subjected to statistical tests, which did show some significant differences pre- and post-intervention. Pupils attributed values as more relevant to the subject curriculum after the interventions. Deakin Crick argues that measuring standards has become an all-consuming policy context but that there is confusion and uncertainty regarding how to measure spiritual and moral development. The key question remains, 'Whose values should the church school seek to develop?'

> *There is a very real danger that evidence from questionnaires only reflects what pupils feel they ought to value.*

Two interview-based studies research the perspectives of Church of England school headteachers in the light of *The Way Ahead* report. Based on interviews with ten Church of England school headteachers, Street's (2007) conclusions are a cause for concern. He argues that the report has had little or no impact on their development of policy and practice. This would suggest that Johnson and McCreery's (1999) findings in relation to primary school headteachers would not be substantially different were the study replicated today (see section 3.2.1). Street (2007) analysed semi-structured questionnaires and drew out three main themes from the headteachers' responses; the themes comprised: i) the value-driven nature of school ethos, ii) the nurture of pupils in the faith and iii) links with the local church. Street found that none of the headteachers were able to differentiate between distinctive Christian values and those held in common with local authority schools. Although all of the headteachers were convinced of the role of their school in nurturing pupils' faith, Street found that they assumed that the holistic life of the school would implicitly impact pupils in terms of faith formation. Street suggests that the reluctance to explicitly link school values to Christianity "may reflect the Church's failure to provide a lead for its teachers in a cultural milieu which considers religion to be an entirely private matter and inappropriate for public consideration" (p. 144). He also writes that, "it is apparent that spirituality remains an elusive concept" (p. 144). Street found that there were few connections between the schools and their local churches. Furthermore, headteachers did not feel that the diocese played much of a proactive role in addressing the nature and purpose of its schools.

> *Frequently voiced criticisms accusing church schools of being culturally divisive are over-simplistic.*

In many ways Colson's (2004) research replicated the Johnson and McCreery (1999) study. He interviewed the headteachers of four voluntary aided Church of England schools in London to investigate their perceptions of their role in the transmission and formation of values. Whilst all of the headteachers identified themselves as being Christian, only two were Anglicans. As in the Johnson and McCreery (1999) study, the headteachers saw themselves as having a significant role in values development but, unlike the previous study, did not perceive external influences such as school governance to be as influential. Colson's study does not fully explore the headteachers' understanding of the role of spirituality in school, but found that the headteachers considered collective worship to be central in both the transmission of values and spiritual development. The four headteachers were concerned to avoid appearing intolerant of the multi-cultural settings in which their schools were located. These two perspectives regarding the role of collective worship and multi-cultural school settings are similar to those articulated by the headteachers in the earlier study (Johnson and McCreery, 1999). Colson (2004) also found that the headteachers regarded the overall purpose of their school to be one of serving the community. He argues that frequently voiced criticisms accusing church schools of being culturally divisive are over-simplistic. Colson suggests that such criticism ignores headteachers' self-understanding of their role in promoting shared values and respecting the multi-ethnic and multi-religious backgrounds of their pupils.

Both Colson's and Street's research appears to demonstrate a lack of clarity in the way that some headteachers understand the distinctiveness of their schools and their role in the transmission of values. It has to be acknowledged, however, that these are small-scale interview studies. In a discussion article, Brown (2003) reviews the implications of opening 100 new Church of England voluntary schools. Brown suggests that *The Way Ahead* report may not hold up the truly inclusive model of service he believes should be at the centre of the church's mission. This discussion appears to reinforce Street's charge that there is ambiguity around the term 'distinctiveness'. Brown attributes this to ecclesiological and theological differences within the Church of England. Colson's and Street's research appears to reaffirm that spirituality and distinctiveness are elusive terms. Brown (2003) describes them as 'slippery as an eel' (p. 111); it is possible that headteachers may lack the vocabulary and the support to fully explore them.

3.2.3 summary

In summary, the majority of research into maintained Church of England schools centres on their impact on attitudes and attainment. In both cases the picture appears to be mixed. The research into pupil attitudes suggests that Church of England schools make a positive contribution to spiritual health in urban areas and that they affirm the religious beliefs of those pupils attending who are Anglicans. But they appear to have a limited impact on the attitude towards religion among the pupils who profess no faith. In relation to achievement there is some evidence that Church of England school pupils do better because of prior attainment although this does not account for all of the difference. The distinctiveness of Church schools is often given as an explanation for this difference but little research has been carried out into the nature of distinctive church school ethos. The qualitative research carried out demonstrates that spirituality, values and distinctiveness are difficult concepts for schools and headteachers to grapple with.

3.3 other Christian maintained schools, comparative studies and faith schools

Johnson (2001) explored the distinctive culture of a voluntary controlled Quaker primary school using documentary analysis of a school prospectus together with interviews.

There is only one voluntary controlled primary school linked to the Religious Society of Friends in England and Wales. The primary school is set in an affluent rural location in the South East of England. None of the pupils attending the school were in receipt of Free School Meals (FSM)[6]; almost all were white and spoke English as their first language. The headteacher of the school was not a Quaker and only two of the pupils came from Quaker families. Johnson wanted to explore whether the school's values were distinguishable from those of a secular state primary school. Johnson found that the prospectus affirmed high standards of behaviour, respect for one another and the intention to instil religious and moral values. Johnson (2001) argues that it is possible to read into the prospectus an emphasis on egalitarianism, justice and friendship consistent with Quaker values. The headteacher of the school confirmed that the emphasis identified by Johnson did represent the values which they sought to promote.

Johnson found, however, that the headteacher did not consider these values to be distinctively Quaker. The evidence from this study seems to suggest that the headteacher and governors saw the relationship with the Religious Society of Friends as largely historical. They were determined that there should be no prosleytisation in the school. The headteacher and governors believed that the

> *Spirituality, values and distinctiveness are difficult concepts for schools and headteachers to grapple with.*

school was popular with parents primarily because of its academic success. Johnson concludes that the lack of overt Quakerism reflects both the small presence of the Quaker community in the population and their openness and tolerance. She writes that the school's educational values were important in and of themselves. Johnson argues that because the school is open about its historical roots in Quakerism it 'has a clear picture of the width and depth of its values' (p. 207).

Johnson (2002) has also researched the distinctive Christian culture of other types of denominational primary schools. As well as interviewing the headteacher of the Quaker primary school, Johnson interviewed the headteachers of six Church of England primary schools and of seven Roman Catholic primary schools. None of the schools were undersubscribed and they were all able to set their own admissions criteria. All of the schools were situated in the same south London diocese. The diocese stretched from inner to outer London and so the schools represented a variety of different social and ethnic communities. The study compared the headteachers' perspectives regarding the transmission of beliefs and values and the creation of a distinctive faith school culture. Johnson conceptualised the way that headteachers derived their role from religious tradition along a spectrum from 'closed to open'. She found that headteachers at the closed end of the spectrum understood it to be their responsibility to shore up traditional religious doctrine, values and expressions of spirituality against the threat of change. She writes that those on the open end of the spectrum showed awareness of contemporary issues and demonstrated the ability to ask questions and to change. Johnson found that headteachers of Roman Catholic schools were more likely to be at the closed end of the spectrum. She places the headteacher of the Quaker school at the open end of the spectrum. The Church of England headteachers could be placed along the spectrum between these two extremes. Johnson found that all of the Church of England headteachers perceived Anglicanism to be a set of liberal values and behaviours. The exception to this was a headteacher who was ordained in the Church of England. She writes that the other headteachers placed little emphasis on the doctrines of the church and 'displayed an ambivalence and uncertainty in the content and process of spiritual and moral development' (p. 217). Johnson's research would seem to concur with Jelfs' conclusion that Church of England primary schools do not fully utilise the opportunity this affords to develop their Christian distinctiveness (see section 3.2.1).

> *Faith schools emphasise the right of parents to choose an education in keeping with their religious views.*

A number of research studies have been carried out which attempt to assess the contribution of maintained faith schools to community cohesion and the nature of their impact on attainment. Although these studies do not exclusively research faith schools of a Christian character, it remains the case that the Christian denominations still dominate maintained provision and so some of the evidence falls within the remit of this review. The Runnymede Trust (Berkely, 2008) commissioned a report into the contribution of faith schools to equality and cohesion in contemporary multi-ethnic society. The trust consulted with over a thousand people, 'including parents, pupils, professionals and policy makers' who came from a range of faith backgrounds as well as those who did not 'subscribe to any religion' (p. 4). The report argues that although faith schools can successfully emphasise the teaching of values, they are more effective at educating 'for a single vision' than engaging in open dialogue on a range of values perspectives (p. 5). The research also found that faith schools emphasise the right of parents to choose an education in keeping with their religious views, despite the fact that parental choice is complex in the current education system, and may be a deliberate act on the part of some to avoid interaction with pupils from other backgrounds. The report thus argued that the schools did not champion the rights of children. It also argued that provision for learning about religion in faith schools was poor, particularly with respect to religions other than that of the sponsoring faith. It was argued that although faith schools have a historic mission to provide for the poor, they educate a disproportionately small number of the most socially and economically deprived pupils today. The report found that inequalities and failure to tackle religious discrimination in non-faith state schools may drive faith school attendance. The report acknowledges that faith is an important facet of human identity and concludes that faith should continue to play a significant role in the education system of England and Wales.

The report made the following six key recommendations (p. 1):

1) End selection on the basis of faith.
2) Children should have a greater say in how they are educated.
3) RE should be part of the core national curriculum.
4) Faith schools should also serve the most disadvantaged.
5) Faith schools must value all young people.
6) Faith should continue to play an important role in the education system.

Pennell, West and Hind (2007) have researched the social composition and admissions policies of state maintained faith schools in London. The research was commissioned by 'Comprehensive Future' in the context of the Labour Government's aim to increase the number of faith-based schools. No information is publicly available about the religion of pupils enrolled in maintained schools with a religious character. This study collected data via a questionnaire that was sent to all voluntary aided and secondary schools with a religious character in London (N=106); 47% of the schools 'provided useable' information (p. 3). Information was also collected on admissions policies including a sample of the supplementary forms that parents are asked to fill in with their application for a place. With respect to religious composition, the research found that although the pupil mix varied, Church of England schools were, overall, more inclusive of other faiths than Roman Catholic schools. In Church of England schools, 'around seven out of ten pupils were reported to be Christian'; in Roman Catholic schools the figure was nine out of ten (p. 1). Pennell *et al.* conclude that those schools which set aside a number of their places for pupils of other faiths/no faith tended to be more inclusive. It should be noted, however, that the most religiously inclusive school in the study did not set aside any of these places. Pennell *et al.* argue that faith schools which were more religiously inclusive were not necessarily inclusive in other areas, particularly in relation to social class. Their analysis of the supplementary forms found that, in all cases, references were required to substantiate the information provided by parents about their religious background and practice. When the faith school supplementary forms were compared to local authority forms they were found to be, in general, more complex. Pennell *et al.* argue that complex supplementary forms together with autonomous admissions criteria allowed, in some cases, the opportunity for schools to socially select pupils.

Gibbons and Silva (2006) have investigated whether faith primary schools raise pupil achievement, 'or whether they simply enrol pupils with characteristics conducive to better educational achievement' (p. 1). They dispute whether any existing studies credibly disentangle these characteristics from school effect. The National Pupil Database (NPD) holds individual pupils' assessment records as well as detailed information such as 'pupils' school, gender, age, ethnicity, language skills, any special educational needs or disabilities and entitlement to free school meals' (p. 11). Gibbons and Silva used information on two cohorts 'who were aged 10-11 and sitting their Key Stage Two tests in 2002 and 2003' (p. 11). The results of their analysis suggest that faith primary schools could offer a very small advantage over secular schools in terms of age 11 test scores in Maths and English. But they argue that the benefits are linked to the more autonomous admission and governance systems in place in voluntary aided schools.

In response to the debate regarding faith schools and social cohesion Godfrey (2009) has conducted a statistical analysis to explore how well faith schools reflect the social composition of local society. This is preliminary work and Godfrey advises that the analysis 'can only set the boundaries for debate rather than offer any real conclusions' (p. 38). The report is based on year 7 pupils admitted to 3201 secondary schools in England in the academic year 2007 – 2008. Godfrey designed an index to show how much more or less likely a school was to accept a pupil in receipt of Free School Meals (see footnote 12) compared to a pupil from a better off family. So far the report confirms 'that on average faith schools take a lower proportion of deprived pupils both from their neighbourhoods and from the wider populations they serve' (p. 38). The analysis also demonstrated that the wider the population a school draws from, the lower the proportion of deprived pupils it is likely to take'. Faith schools are more likely to draw from wider populations than non-faith schools. Godfrey found that Church of England schools outside of London and the North West which drew from wider populations were more likely to take FSM pupils than other schools. In London the correlation with non-faith schools was higher and in the North West it was about the same. Clearly the picture is complex and more analysis is needed.

3.3.1 summary

In summary, the comparative studies of schools with a Christian ethos suggest that headteachers perceive Christian distinctiveness in a variety of ways depending on their own context and personal attitude towards religion. This evidence also demonstrates a lack of clarity with respect to terms like spirituality, values education and Christian ethos. Similarly, the research on faith schools demonstrates that researchers hold a range of views on the desirability of faith schools, their distinctiveness and the nature of spirituality, inclusiveness and values education. The argument that faith schools should be more inclusive assumes that religious schools which conceptualise their distinctiveness in confessional terms are divisive. The research on religious schools and attainment demonstrated once again how difficult it is to disentangle the effects of home, church and school on pupil performance.

chapter 3 - references

1. The 'Religion and Values Today' project sought to profile the values of young people between the ages of 13 and 15. The project administered a revised version of the Centymca Attitude Inventory (Francis, 1982, 1984a, 1984b, Francis & Kay, 1995). Using a Likert scaling, pupils are asked to grade their agreement with short focussed statements on a five point scale. The instrument has been designed to profile values across fifteen areas. These comprise: personal well-being, worries, counselling, school, work, religious beliefs, church and society, the supernatural, politics, social concerns, sexual morality, substance use, right and wrong, leisure and the local area.

2. General Certificate of Secondary Education.

3. Office for Standards in Education.

4. The Effective Lifelong Learning Inventory is a self-assessed learning questionnaire designed by Deakin Crick, Broadfoot & Claxton (2004) to find out how learners perceive themselves in relation to key dimensions of learning power (see http://www.ellionline.co.uk).

5. The repertory grid is an instrument developed by Kelly (1955) for use within personal construct psychology research. A personal construct system consists of a 'developed set of representations or models of the world' (Deakin Crick, 2002, p. 24). The repertory grid is a form of structured interview designed to elicit and analyse the subjects' personal construct systems. In the case of Deakin Crick's research, core constructs were analysed in relation to school to elicit the working worldviews of teachers and pupils. The grid has two axes. The vertical axis comprised elements representing different aspects of the school and the horizontal axis represented the different ways that subjects construed these elements (p. 27).

6. Eligibility for Free School Meals is a widely accepted indicator of social deprivation.

independent schools in England

4.1 city technology colleges and academies

City Technology Colleges (CTCs) and Academies are technically independent schools. Business, industry and/or charitable foundations sponsoring CTCs and Academies make an initial investment but receive *per capita* funding from the government. According to Curtis (2009), 38 of the 133 Academies open at the time of writing are sponsored by faith-based organisations, and a further 13 co-sponsored by faith-based organisations. CTCs were a Conservative Government initiative of the 1980s, designed to address the particular challenges of urban deprivation by creating local partnerships of investment and sponsorship to deliver education (Green, 2009b). The current Labour Government has embraced and developed the principles behind CTCs and used them as a model for its Academies programme (DfES, 2005, p. 3). To date, Green (forthcoming) has conducted the only research into a CTC with a Christian ethos. Emmanuel CTC is sponsored by Sir Peter Vardy's Emmanuel Schools Foundation (ESF). The ESF is committed to sponsoring a further seven Academies in the North East of England, two of which are already open and a third due to open in September 2009. Pike (2009) has conducted a small case-study at Trinity Academy sponsored by the ESF; Trinity Academy opened in 2006. Research into Academies is in its early stages; this reflects the fact that most of them have only opened within the last three to five years.

Green's (forthcoming) research at Emmanuel CTC utilised ethnographic methodology to describe and analyse the relationship between a highly intentional Christian ethos, described by the ESF as 'Bible-based', and the culture of pupils. Ethnographic work is by no means subject to generalisation, but the point about Emmanuel CTC is that it represented a unique case. Emmanuel is the only CTC to be funded by a non-denominational Christian foundation. There is one other CTC with a Christian foundation, which is co-sponsored by the Church of England. When the fieldwork for the study was carried out in 2007, Emmanuel CTC had a GCSE A*-C pass rate of 99%; the national average was 60.3%. The CTC policy was designed to raise achievement and increase opportunities in areas of urban deprivation and so, on the face of it, Emmanuel CTC would seem to have been very effective. It is the vision of the CTC's sponsor, Sir Peter Vardy, that ESF schools should raise achievement and contribute to community regeneration within a moral and ethical framework that is broadly Christian. This framework is expressed in seven core values, regarded by the ESF as central to their vision and ethos. These core values comprise:

1) Honourable purpose
2) Humility
3) Compassion
4) Integrity
5) Accountability
6) Courage
7) Determination
   (Emmanuel Schools Foundation, 2007)

Green's study found that the sponsors and senior staff at Emmanuel CTC shared a theologically conservative Christian worldview, and that the assumptions embedded in this worldview shaped decision making, policies, authority and discipline structures and the nature of Bible teaching. Bible teaching was seen as a central mechanism for the delivery of ethos in assemblies and in tutor times (referred to by the ESF as 'tutor prayers', see Green, 2009c). The core values of the school, somewhat surprisingly, are not expressed in religious terms. Green (2009b) and Pike (2009) both argue that core values can be seen as a consensual space where different conceptions of the origins of values and morality i.e. the Bible or elsewhere, can coalesce. Pike (2009) argues that the core values facilitate a form of character education founded in Christian faith and values. In this he rehearses Arthur's (2003) contention that schools with a Christian ethos may offer a deeper foundation for character education than secular schools because of the 'Christian sense of forgiveness, grace, love, hope, faith and humility' (p.

> *Core values can be seen as a consensual space where different conceptions of the origins of values and morality can coalesce.*

148). In contrast Green (2009a) makes the case that expressing core values in this way has the practical effect of diluting the Christian basis of the ethos being communicated to pupils. Green found that, with the exception of RE, Christian content was largely absent from the curriculum. She argues that this creates the impression that the Bible is only relevant to particular cultural spaces, and reinforces the view she found commonly expressed by pupils, that it was not relevant outside of the private sphere. Emmanuel Foundation schools are well known for their strict discipline and traditional pedagogy (Paton, 2007). Green (forthcoming) argues that the view of religious knowledge presented to pupils within the CTC and Academies belongs within a modernist apologetics framework. This presents religious truth as authoritative and factual, to be weighed up and either accepted or rejected. She suggests that this may clash with the views of knowledge embedded more widely in the cultural paradigm of the pupils, who are more inclined to accept things as 'true' when they closely connect to personal history and experience. The research found that although pupils demonstrated good biblical knowledge and valued being informed about religion, there was little evidence that the Bible-based ethos was a strong enough vehicle to radically reshape their worldview. Green concludes that a clash of knowledge paradigms helps to account for this. She also argues that institutional structures filter the Christian worldview of the sponsor and senior staff so that, in the experience of pupils, it is no longer presented as a worldview but experienced as a symbolic power, or a set of cultural expectations.

Pike (2009) has investigated the relationship between the ESF's core values, private business sponsorship, Christian ethos and the high aspirations for pupils at Trinity Academy. Trinity Academy 'was designated the most improved academy nationally and the most improved school in Yorkshire and Humberside' (Pike, 2009, p. 139). It replaced a predecessor community school serving the social priority areas of Thorne and Moorend. The percentage of pupils attaining five or more GCSE grades A* to C at Trinity Academy has risen from 34 in 2006, to 74 in 2008. Pike adopted a case study design for his research at Trinity Academy. Data was collected via interview, questionnaires, lesson observation and documentary analysis. Three interviews were conducted with the sponsor, Sir Peter Vardy, and an anonymous survey was administered to Year Nine pupils. Pike found that the sponsor's vision was not simply to improve individual schools but to improve education and stimulate community regeneration.

> *Sir Peter Vardy built into his business model a focus on developing personal qualities such as courtesy and respect.*

Pike notes that this improvement and regeneration should not simply be understood in terms of profit and academic achievement. Sir Peter Vardy built into his business model a focus on developing the personal qualities that he prized, such as courtesy and respect. This emphasis on character development has been translated into ESF Academies via the set of core values. Pike found that 'shared core values form the basis of the emphasis on good character at Trinity Academy' (p. 140). He writes that '96% of 191 14-year-olds agreed that their school's core values were good values to have and most, if not all, of the teachers interviewed endorsed and approved of them' (p. 140). Pike argues that the evidence from Trinity lends credence to the argument that character development promotes academic achievement. Furthermore, he writes that the Christian ethos directly underpins the high aspirations for pupils found at Trinity Academy because the ESF views all children as being made in God's image. Pike argues that this Christian view of the value of the person is fundamental to the desire of the Foundation to improve the opportunities for pupils who live in the social priority area served by the Academy. Pike anticipates the argument that generalisations from a case study may not be regarded as valid. He concludes that because Trinity Academy is the only school serving the communities of Thorne and Moorend, and because it does not select on the basis of faith, attitude or aptitude, a credible case can be made for the significance of business sponsorship, core values and Christian ethos in transforming the opportunities for pupils.

4.1.1 summary

In summary, although the ESF is one of the biggest Christian organisations sponsoring a CTC and Academies, it is not necessarily representative of the wider field. The research demonstrates that the ESF has a theology and pedagogy particular to their organisation and Christian worldview. The evidence from ethnography and case study research seems to suggest that they are successful in terms of academic achievement. But these studies do not disentangle the impact of home, church and school. More research would be needed to demonstrate what the nature of the impact on character development might consist of and to establish whether it is indeed related to the academic achievement of pupils. More research is needed to explore the models being developed in church-sponsored Academies and by other Christian sponsors.

4.2 independent schools

This review found two notable strands of research into independent schools with a Christian ethos. The first of these concerns what this review has termed 'traditional independent schools' often with an affiliation to the Church of England. The National Society estimated the number to be around 200 in 2007 (p. 4). The Bloxham Project exists as an umbrella organisation for many of these schools and promotes in-house training, reflection and research for schools and their chaplains. Although their research is in the public domain it has not been subject to an academic peer review process. The second strand concerns what Walford (1995) described as the 'new Christian schools'. These tend to be small, parent-controlled schools, some of which are affiliated to evangelical or charismatic free churches, although many are independent of church organisations. Their history has been chronicled by Deakin (1989), by Baker and Freeman (2005) and by Walford (1991, 2001). As with the traditional independent sector, it is hard to determine precisely how many such schools there are. The Christian Schools Trust (CST), an umbrella organisation representing some of the new Christian schools, had 47 schools listed in their directory in 2007. The problem with both of these strands of research is that they tend to group diverse institutions together when they report their findings. This is understandable given the limited amount of evidence available, but still problematic.

The Bloxham Project (2008, 2007) has published two discussion papers related to spirituality among young people and as a dimension of school leadership. In addition, the project circulates presentations and papers given at Bloxham conferences and training days which comment on the theme of spirituality and promoting Christian values in school. Whilst these papers do not constitute empirical research, taken as a whole, they are indicative of the ways schools associated with Bloxham are exploring the notion of Christian distinctiveness, particularly in relation to Christian identity, character formation and spirituality. One significant theme is the impact of the church and church schools on a society in which concepts of religious truth and spirituality are changing (Acheson, 2003, Kirby, 2004). This was also found to be an important theme in the research on maintained Church of England schools (see chapter 3, section 2). Another significant theme is the question of what it means to be a church school. Authors of Bloxham papers such as Acheson (2003) and Adams (2004) raise questions about the extent to which their individual schools are communities in which Christian values are being lived out. Adams (2004) argues that church schools need to develop a clearer educational idea of the nature of the person (p. 1). In common with Jelfs (2008), he argues that contemporary concepts of education are too functional, too preoccupied with academic attainment and that a fuller, more relational view of the person and education is required.

> *Contemporary concepts of education are too preoccupied with academic attainment and a more relational view is required.*

In addition to the perspective offered by the Bloxham papers, the review found a research study by Gay (2000) reporting pupils' reflections on the religious dimensions of their school. The study begins by investigating the problem of the term 'spiritual development' before reporting on the findings of a questionnaire. The questionnaire was administered to 287 Year Seven pupils and 231 Year Ten pupils in 17 independent girls' schools. The schools were affiliated to the Church of England and members either of the Headmasters' Conference or of the Girls' Schools Association. Gay arrived at a working definition which assumed that spiritual development encompassed the development of 'beliefs, values, self-knowledge, awareness of others' and the ability to reflect on one's environment, and ask questions about the transcendent (p. 63). It is interesting that this definition comprises a similar range to that encompassed by Fisher *et al's* (2000) four domains of spiritual well-being (personal, communal, environmental and transcendent). Gay found that collective acts of worship and school ethos did appear, from the perspective of pupils, to develop self-knowledge by enabling them to feel part of a community. Forty-eight per cent of Year Seven pupils and 44% of Year Ten pupils saw religion as having a positive effect on teaching and behaviour in school (p. 72). In relation to their own attitudes, values and beliefs 53% of Year Seven pupils and 62% of Year Ten pupils said that school had had a positive effect. Gay attempts to unpack what they meant by this. She argues that most of the pupils understood this effect in terms of the positive way school had influenced their values and behaviour. The pupils did not feel that school had strengthened their own religious beliefs. Only 10.4% of Year Seven pupils and 11.6% of Year Ten pupils felt that the religious dimension of school life had helped to increase their religious understanding and enable them to reflect on theological and moral issues (p. 73). Gay acknowledges that this is a small exploratory study, and that a fuller investigation is needed of the ways in which spiritual development may be fostered across school structures such as the curriculum and in the nurturing of imaginative and creative capacities among pupils (p. 74). This work is clearly too small and too exploratory to be able to generalise from the findings, but it does offer a significant attempt to theorise the concept of spiritual development.

As part of the teenage religion and values project, Francis (2001) surveyed the attitudes of pupils at independent Christian schools. Nineteen such schools participated in the project, but Francis does not specify how many of these could be described as 'new Christian schools' and so we must assume that the results reported may well comprise a diverse range of independent schools. Francis (2005) has compared the values of 12,823 boys attending non-denominational schools with 136 boys attending independent Christian schools. He concludes that, 'the values environment modelled by the 13-15 year old boys attending Christian schools is significantly different from that modelled by boys' attending the non-denominational schools (p. 241). The study found that boys attending the Christian schools shared a much higher level of religious belief in God. Furthermore, Francis writes that the kind of God these boys believed in was 'fashioned by biblical fundamentalism' (p. 236). Eighty-two per cent of the boys attending Christian schools believed that God made the world in six days and rested on the seventh; 67% of the boys believed that Christianity was the only true religion (p. 238). The boys attending Christian schools reported more positive attitudes towards the church and the Bible, and more commitment towards hard work and alleviating social concerns, and they were less likely to hold superstitious beliefs or to condone smoking and drinking. The boys did not, however, present a uniform view either on sexual ethics or on substance use and they were no more likely than boys attending non-denominational schools to project a uniformly law-abiding profile. Francis concludes that the values environment being modelled by the boys at Christian schools is indeed 'more Christian' than can be found in the non-denominational state maintained schools. Clearly more research is needed to unpack precisely what this means.

> *Boys attending Christian schools reported more positive attitudes towards the church and the Bible, more commitment towards hard work and alleviating social concerns.*

As part of the 'Urban Hope and Spiritual Health Project', Francis and Robbins (2005) also reported findings in relation to pupils attending independent Christian schools serving urban communities. Francis compared pupils educated in independent Christian schools with those educated in non-denominational schools. Within the personal domain, pupils at independent Christian schools signalled better spiritual health on a number of measures. Fewer independent Christian school pupils reported feeling depressed or said that they had considered suicide compared with pupils at non-denominational schools. Seventy-five per cent of pupils at Christian schools said that they felt they had a sense of purpose in life compared with 52% of pupils attending non-denominational schools. There were no significant differences between pupils on the other indicators of spiritual health in the personal domain. With respect to the communal domain, pupils at Christian schools were less likely to be worried about bullying at school and more likely to get help from talking to their friends. But they were also more likely to be worried about getting on with others and less likely to like the people with whom they went to school. Francis found that in the environmental and transcendental domains, pupils at Christian schools enjoyed a significantly higher level of spiritual health. He concludes that there are significant ways across all four domains in which pupils at Christian schools enjoy a higher level of spiritual health compared with pupils at non-denominational schools.

Francis, Ap Sion and Baker (Ap Sion *et al.*, 2007, Francis *et al.*, in press) have adopted an individual differences approach, using a methodology derived from empirical theology, to evaluate the impact of the new Christian schools upon their pupils. This owes much to the individual differences approach found in psychology. This assumes that human behaviour is not random, but patterned, and that core factors such as gender can predict difference. Francis (in press) argues that religion is a powerful predictor of attitudes and behaviour. The individual differences approach within empirical theology roots individual difference in the doctrine of creation. Arguing that God has created individual difference such as gender, ethnicity and personality, this empirical theological approach researches the ways in which religion is associated with the variety of these differences 'central to human personal and social functioning' (p. 128). Two published studies present evidence from questionnaires carried out among the population of male and female graduates respectively who attended the new Christian schools and left between 1985 and 2003 (Ap Sion *et al.*, 2007, Francis *et al.*, in press). The questionnaires administered comprised a combination of open and closed questions designed to elicit the reflections of graduates upon their school experience. These included some focussed questions around whether graduates felt they had enjoyed school, whether they felt overprotected and whether they had been prepared for the next stage of education/work (Ap Sion *et al.*, 2007, p. 1). The responses were analysed in relation to four themes derived from Baker and Freeman's (2005) account of the aspirations and goals of the new Christian schools for their pupils. The four themes were:

> **Pupils at Christian schools enjoy a higher level of spiritual health compared with pupils at non-denominational schools.**

1) The quality of the education.
2) The context of Christian and moral nurture.

3) The quality of relationships (pupils, teachers and wider world).
4) Preparation received for life after leaving school.

In relation to the first theme, quality of education, the study of male graduates found that pupils mostly referred to the high academic standards in their schools. In addition, some criticisms were made about what had been possible due to the size of the school. In some cases this seems to have impacted things like the number of subjects that could be taken at examination level and the availability of specialist subject teachers. Responses from female graduates concur with these findings. Female graduates also commented that other subjects should have featured more highly in the curriculum, including teaching on other religions, sex, drugs and alcohol. Only one male graduate raised this as a concern. Both studies conclude that most of the comments from male and female graduates on the theme of Christian and moral nurture appear to be positive. They present evidence from individual respondents who reflected positively on the way in which school reinforced the Christian principles of home and provided opportunities to develop in their faith. Francis *et al.* (in press) also wrote, however, that many female graduates made 'negative comments' regarding the quality and consequences of 'Christian aspects' of school and 'pupils' faith development':

> *This research provides important evidence of how the new Christian schools may understand their mission and the kind of impact they desire to have upon their pupils.*

> [M]ost of these comments referred to schools' emphasis on external image and conformity, lack of opportunity for internal, individual spiritual development, 'spoon feeding' of ideas or coercion, restricted opportunities for self-expression, difficulty living one's faith, and the need to engage with real issues (p. 232).

This does not entirely fit with the claim that most of the comments relating to Christian and moral nurture amongst female graduates were positive. This probably reflects how difficult it is to put a comprehensive picture together from individual responses that may not neatly fit within themes. Without knowing how many comments were positive or negative it is difficult to judge whether this is indeed a conflict in the evidence. With respect to the third theme, 'quality of relationships', responses from male and female graduates were positive in relation to pupil-to-pupil and pupil-to-teacher relationships, but less so in relation to the outside world. Female graduates mentioned small class sizes, positive ethos and caring teachers when accounting for high quality relationships, although there were some female graduates who remembered bullying incidents and some male graduates who did not feel they entirely fitted in with the family atmosphere.

The fourth theme to be analysed was the extent to which the graduates felt that their education had prepared them for life beyond school. The studies concluded that both male and female graduates felt well prepared. Some male and female graduates did report experiencing difficulties in transition; they mention increased workload or being unprepared to encounter swearing, drugs, alcohol and pornography. Both studies conclude overall that the evidence demonstrates that the new Christian schools are performing well in relation to the four themes. This research provides important evidence of how the new Christian schools may understand their mission and the kind of impact they desire to have upon their pupils. The reflections of pupils provide an indication of how their attitudes and values may have been shaped, but they do not constitute a definitive picture of the impact of the new Christian schools on beliefs, attitudes, behaviours and spiritual development.

4.2.1 summary

In summary, it is impossible to draw a meaningful picture about the impact of independent schools with a Christian ethos from the evidence summarised here. The summaries demonstrate that small inroads have been made into research in this area, but that widely different methodological approaches have been undertaken within different research traditions, ranging from sociology to empirical theology. This does reconfirm that there is wide variety of proxy terms used to research schools with a Christian ethos and very different understandings of terms like 'spirituality' employed within the studies.

international studies

The studies included in this chapter constitute only a small sample of the international research. They offer a perspective which suggests that there is some continuity in terms of focus and agenda. The research predominately relates to the English-speaking world although some European studies published in English have been included (see section 2.1 for selection criteria). The methodologies employed in these studies are diverse and the research covers a wide range of school types. It may be an obvious point, but it is worth stating that the school types in this research do not directly correspond to those in England and Wales previously reviewed. For ease of reference the studies have been grouped according to country first and then by school type.

5.1 Australasia

The Australian government has systematically funded non-state schools nationwide, since 1973 (Glenn and De Groof, 2002). In 2000, approximately 30% of pupils attended subsidised non-government schools. Twenty per cent of the school age population attends subsided Catholic schools. Protestant schools fall into six categories: i) ACE schools, ii) Christian Parent Controlled Schools (CPCS), iii) Christian Community Schools Ltd (CCSL), iv) Christian City Colleges (CCC), v) Anglican schools often linked with the Australian Anglican Schools Network (AASN) and vi) other schools which do not affiliate to these five umbrella groups.

5.1.1 Catholic schools in Australasia

McLaughlin's (2005) research is predicated on statistics demonstrating that Catholic education is becoming a popular commodity among Australian parents of other faiths and none. As in the UK and US, Catholic education in Australia has a historic commitment to provide nurture in the Catholic faith and education for the poor. McLaughlin's study analyses previous research into the attitudes of parents, pupils and teachers towards traditional Catholic church teaching and doctrine. In this respect it forms a helpful introduction to the current research, although it also establishes that it is limited in its scope. He uses the findings to frame a discussion around the relevance of the traditional model of Catholic education to contemporary pluralist society in Australia. McLaughlin presents evidence to show that the vast majority of parents sending their children to Catholic schools 'either do not practise Catholicism or are not Catholics' (p. 218). He also points out that they are not poor, citing fees as the main deterrent for disadvantaged families. McLaughlin argues that these parents are seeking the high educational standards and human values experienced in Catholic schools but not committing themselves to the formal practice of Catholicism (p. 218). In support of this argument, McLaughlin cites an extensive survey administered to the parents of Catholic school pupils (Sultmann *et al.*, 2003). This survey found that the quality of teaching, care of children and school discipline constituted the main reasons cited by parents for choosing a Catholic school. McLaughlin notes that Arthur and Godfrey (2005) make a similar case for the popularity of Catholic schools among non-Catholic parents in the UK. McLaughlin summarises two recent studies that surveyed the beliefs and attitudes of school-age Catholic pupils: i) Flynn and Mok (2000) and ii) the Australian Bishops' National Life Survey (Dixon, 2004). It should be noted that in drawing conclusions McLaughlin is sometimes unclear as to whether he is talking about pupils attending Catholic schools as a whole, Catholics attending Catholic schools or Catholic pupils as a whole (regardless of whether they were attending a Catholic school or not). The Flynn and Mok (2000) and Dixon (2004)

> *The current model of Catholic education does not offer a spirituality that is perceived by pupils as relevant to the way that they live their lives.*

surveys found a decline in orthodox belief among Catholic pupils. For example, although pupils attending Catholic school said that they believed in God, most were unclear about 'the meaning of God', with only half of practising Catholic pupils expressing the Trinity 'as a dominant image' (McLaughlin, 2005, p. 222). Similarly, only 33% of Catholic pupils accepted Jesus' humanity and only 20% accepted unconditionally the church's teaching on abortion (p. 223). McLaughlin argues that the current model of Catholic education does not offer a spirituality that is perceived by pupils as relevant to the way that they live their lives. This study affirms that there are similar trends in Australia as in the UK regarding the popularity of Catholic schools among parents, and an educational discourse centred on high standards of attainment and discipline.

The SESI research paradigm has been influential on the educational policy discourse in Australia. This is illustrated in the database by an address given to the Australian Anglican Schools Network (AASN) by Michael Chaney (2008). Chaney was chair of the governing body of John XXIII College, a Catholic school in Perth. His address summarises the school's approach to spiritual development within the context of organisational culture and management. Chaney disagrees with the common charge levied against SESI approaches that schools cannot be run like businesses. He describes how a positive change in school culture was effected by the use of a corporate planning system called the 'Argenti Planning system'. Chaney (2008) argues that the adoption of a strategic planning approach prevented decisions from being made in a vacuum, particularly those that related to the vision the school had for its pupils. The governors of the school were asking, 'Were our pupils really living the Gospel?' In a collaborative process, the governors and staff at John XXIII developed the following objective: 'our College seeks to develop people of competence, conscience and compassion, who are committed to God and the service of others'. Arguably, these are goals directly associated with the spiritual development of pupils, but traditionally considered difficult to measure objectively. Chaney argues that psychologists have developed measures able to

> *This exercise suggests that spirituality and other non-affective cognitive characteristics can be measured.*

cope with non-cognitive or affective characteristics long used by employers. These instruments make it possible to measure whether pupils are developing academic, social and emotional competence. Chaney does not, however, detail in his address which instruments were employed to measure these objectives. Nevertheless this exercise raises an important issue relating to the impact of schools with a Christian ethos on the spiritual development of pupils. It suggests that spirituality and other non-affective cognitive characteristics can be measured. This in turn raises a question in relation to measurement and target setting. Is it desirable for schools to measure impact in this way and is it appropriate to set whole school, or individual, targets for spiritual development?

Chaney's definition of spirituality appears to be closely tied to a traditional religious understanding of spiritual development, conceptualised as effectively living out gospel values. A very different approach is in evidence in Hyde's (2008) research. Hyde conducted one of the very first studies in Australia of children's spirituality in the context of Catholic primary schools. The aim was to identify some characteristics of spirituality among primary school pupils. Hyde's definition of spirituality stems from a post-modern, research paradigm, in which it is argued that educators should not impose a narrative upon children as they develop their sense of spirituality in relation to their own experience. He thus uses hermeneutic phenomenology as a theoretical approach. This approach attempts to treat children's lives and experiences as a text. Hyde spent five weeks in three Catholic primary schools, one in the inner city, one in the suburbs and one in a rural location. Two small groups of children (six pupils aged eight, and six aged ten) were selected from each school. Small group meetings were guided by three categories for spiritual sensitivity outlined by Hay and Nye (2006). These comprise: i) awareness sensing, ii) mystery sensing and iii) value sensing. The meetings formed the main 'texts' from which Hyde identified characteristics of the children's spirituality. Hyde found that the children's sense of wonder drew on the different frameworks of meaning, cultural traditions and worldviews within which they had been brought up. Despite being immersed in a school context which promoted a Catholic worldview, the children appeared to draw on an eclectic range of concepts and ideas to form their own personal framework of meaning. Hyde argues that although the children were influenced by the cultural, religious and social contexts of meaning around them, they were nonetheless exercising individual choice in 'weaving together' their 'own threads of meaning' (p. 241).

Kennedy and Duncan (2006) raise similar issues in the context of New Zealand Catholic primary schools. Researching teachers' perspectives on spirituality in Catholic schools, they found an increasing awareness of spirituality in relation to the context of pupils' lives. In New Zealand, primary and secondary schools are either wholly secular or 'integrated'. Integrated schools in the state system have a specialist character which defines a particular educational philosophy and the vast majority of such schools have a religious affiliation. Catholic primary schools form the biggest group of integrated primary schools in New Zealand. Many of the primary schools were originally formed by religious orders but the vast majority are currently staffed by lay Catholics or by teachers from other faiths and none. Kennedy and Duncan (2006) write that, 'an important part of the special character of Catholic schools involves nurturing the spirituality of children' (p. 283). The expectation is that this will be done within a religious framework that reflects Catholic tradition. Kennedy and Duncan (2006) demonstrated that teachers in the Catholic schools studied did understand spirituality from within a religious framework. They concluded that this did not limit the ways in which they experienced spirituality and recognised 'children's spiritual expressions' (p. 291). Kennedy and Duncan argue that the essential component of what makes schools 'Catholic' is that they provide an environment in which children's spirituality is recognised and nurtured. They affirm that the root of this climate lies in traditional religious notions of spirituality but need not be restricted to this. Kennedy and Duncan are arguing that religious notions of spirituality may affirm wider concepts of well-being without compromising children's individuality and experience.

5.1.2 Protestant schools in Australia

Research into Protestant schools in Australia has also been influenced by the SESI research paradigm. Australian Protestant schools are normally autonomous organisations which are affiliated to national or state-based umbrella groups. Independent of government administration, they do, however, receive some subsidy in the form of per capita recurrent grants which provide a high proportion of running costs (Twelves, 2001, p. 61). Twelves (2001) carried out case study research into three Australian Protestant schools considered to be successful. He interviewed senior leaders in the schools using a structured schedule designed to establish their style of leadership and management practices. The three schools all had primary and secondary departments, had all been open for approximately 20 years and had total enrolments of between 600 and 800 pupils. Twelves found that the leaders of the schools did not attribute success to their personal leadership style, but to collaborative approaches which had moved away from more traditional bureaucratic and hierarchical models. All three schools had moved to governance models in which the Principal had more autonomy, functioning more like a Chief Executive. The schools exhibited greater diversity in relation to enrolment policies. Twelves concluded therefore that operating a closed or open enrolment policy was unrelated to success. He argued that sticking to an agreed enrolment policy was the crucial factor in achieving success. All the leaders interviewed cited high quality teaching staff as the 'prime factor' in their success (p. 69). All three schools insisted on unequivocal Christian commitment from all their teachers. The leaders interviewed felt this had a significant impact on the lives of their pupils, citing the transformation observed in their lives. They believed that this could be measured by the positive Christian difference pupils would make in communities during their adult life. Two of the schools felt that they could already demonstrate success in this area; the third school felt that it could not. Twelves acknowledges that, 'the lack of any published detailed research on specifically Christian pupil outcomes hinders any meaningful judgements being reached' (p. 71). All three schools considered review and strategic planning to be very significant in their success. What is notable about this study is that Twelves does not view the notion of success in relation to Christian ethos schooling as a problem. Collier and Dowson (2007) have done so in their research into the quality and effectiveness of Christian education.

> **A highly didactic approach to evangelism may result in poor pedagogy and disaffection among pupils with respect to the Christian gospel.**

Collier and Dowson (2007) believe that the primary function of teachers in a Christian school is to educate. They are not arguing that evangelism is incompatible with education. Rather they assume that education and evangelism are mutually contradictory in their aims if evangelism results in the suppression of debate and 'insulates pupils from engagement with the world' (p. 28). They argue that a highly didactic approach to evangelism may result in poor pedagogy and disaffection among pupils with respect to the Christian gospel. They also assume that it will be difficult for teachers and schools to perceive that their approach is closed rather than open. These issues were researched via longitudinal case study and an intervention in one inclusive and interdenominational Christian school in Sydney, Australia. The school has 1350 pupils; whilst it has no religious tests of entry and accepts pupils 'of any or no faith', it does expect teachers to be 'active members of a Christian faith community' (p. 29). The programme of research comprised three interrelated studies. For the first study, 12 senior pupils were interviewed in focus groups and asked for their perceptions of their schooling and the nature of the curriculum. The 12 pupils were prefects and they were interviewed just prior to their final term. They were chosen because they were pupil leaders in their final year of schooling and thus could reflect articulately on their six years' experience of attending the school. The dominant themes in the pupils' responses were: i) hostility ii) boredom and iii) the quashing of dissent. As a result of these findings it was decided to survey all of the pupils in Year 12 (N=120) to see if these perceptions were widely shared. This second study confirmed that these criticisms were widely shared by pupils. Collier and Dowson concluded that there 'was strong consensus that pupils had effectively been counter-evangelised by the school's Christian Education programme' (p. 33). On the basis of these findings the school implemented a number of measures to reorganise the Christian Education programme. These measures comprised:

1) Staff training to maintain openness to the Christian message among pupils even if they remained unconvinced by it when they left school.
2) Staff training to provide cognitive space and metacognitive support to pupils in order to enable them to incorporate new perspectives into their view of reality.
3) Organisation of retreats and conferences to give staff reflective space.
4) A new course of school induction.
5) Formation of a formal partnership with a University so that teachers could study accredited courses in Christian Education.
6) Commitment to particular curriculum initiatives which targeted teaching about the Christian message more specifically to the pupils' own context.
7) Establishing a Christian perspectives committee whose job it was to establish benchmarks for course development in Christian Education.

The effectiveness of this intervention was evaluated in study three. Another survey was carried out among Year 12 pupils and their responses demonstrated that 'opposition to the school's presentation of the Christian message had dropped from 70% of Year 12 (1999) to 30% (2004)' (p. 35). Collier and Dowson argue that this targeted action research project demonstrates that evangelism in school is more likely to be effective if the approaches are less confrontational and more pedagogically sound.

5.1.3 comparative studies in Australia

Fisher's concept of spiritual health has informed Francis' research into denominational schools in England (Fisher, 1999, 2004, 2008, Fisher et al., 2000). Fisher's instrument was developed in Australia and he uses it to report on pupils' perceptions of the impact of denominational schooling in Australia on their spiritual health (Fisher, 2006). Fisher surveyed 1002 secondary school pupils, aged between 12 and 18, in Catholic, Christian community schools and other independent schools in Victoria, Australia. Fisher's measure asks for two responses: each person's ideal for the items within the four domains (personal, communal, environmental and transcendent), and their lived experience. This enables conclusions to be drawn about the level of dissonance between the ideal and the lived experience. High dissonance between the two would be evidence of poorer spiritual well-being. Fisher found that Catholic pupils were the most idealistic and 'reported the highest lived experience in the personal domain' (p. 351). The independent school pupils reported the lowest lived experience in the personal domain. Christian community school pupils were more idealistic in the communal domain, but Fisher found there to be no significant differences between the school types for lived experience in the communal domain. In the environmental domain, Catholic pupils reported higher ideal and lived experiences, followed by independent school pupils. Christian community school pupils reported the lowest ideal and lived experience for the environmental domain. In the transcendental domain, however, Christian community school pupils reported the highest ideal and lived experiences. Independent school pupils reported the lowest ideal and lived experience within the transcendental domain.

> *As pupils aged they moved away from the religious belief system of their school.*

Fisher found that nearly 10% of the pupils, regardless of school type, reported a marked dissonance in the personal domain of spiritual well-being. He also found that more Christian school pupils recorded dissonance in the communal domain than pupils in other types of school. His analysis also demonstrates that as pupils in all types of school moved from the junior to secondary level, they were much more likely to report dissonance between the beliefs about God they ideally expressed and their lived experience. In other words, as pupils aged they moved away from the religious belief system of their school. Fisher's measure cannot demonstrate the causes of these reported differences. This means that we do not know from this evidence what it is about the different school types that may impact pupil perceptions about their spiritual health. What the evidence does demonstrate is that pupils in Christian ethos secondary schools appear to be less likely to be impacted by the religious belief system of their school. This presents schools with an important question about how relevant, or effective, their existing approaches to spiritual development may be. Fisher is recommending a much more holistic approach to the issue of spiritual development. He is also arguing, as Chaney does (2008), that pupils' spiritual development, or health, can be measured. This lends support to the argument that spiritual development can be managed within whole school strategic planning.

5.1.4 summary

To summarise, these research examples seem to suggest that schools with a Christian ethos in Australasia are facing similar challenges to those in the UK. All of the studies deal in some way with defining or redefining the mission of Christian ethos education in contemporary society. They focus specifically on how to define spirituality and how to measure if Christian ethos schools have an impact on their pupils' spiritual development. As in the UK, schools and researchers pose these questions, and the possible solutions, in relation to their paradigms of knowledge.

5.2 Europe

The research presented in this section offers a very small sample of the research carried out in Europe and may only be taken as an example of the focus and themes. The majority of the studies relate to the Netherlands. In the Netherlands, schools with a Christian ethos are routinely funded by the state. This policy is significant because it has influenced debate over the funding of faith schools in the UK, offering a possible policy model to schools and to politicians seeking state funding for schools with special character.

5.2.1 Belgium

Belgium has three separate school systems based on its three language communities: Flemish, German and French. In all systems, private schools have the right to state subsidy, the majority of schools being in reality either secular or Catholic (Glenn and de Groof, 2002). Pugh and Telhaj (2008) have used data from the Trends in Mathematics and Science Study (TIMSS R, 1999)[2] to explore the theory that faith schools have a positive effect on pupil attainment because they create higher social capital. The use of the TIMSS R data is significant, because the comparison of pupil performance by country and by school type has been extremely influential in setting policy agendas in the participating countries in relation to mathematics and science. Pugh and Telhaj's (2008) results suggest that when influenced by faith communities, schools have a modest effect on attainment in mathematics but that this is not the case when schools are influenced by trade unions and business groups. Furthermore they found that positive attainment in faith schools was not the result of selection bias but reflected forms of social capital more available in faith schools than non-faith schools. TIMSS R data, however, does not provide information about prior attainment or prior schooling, so Pugh and Telhaj's results do not demonstrate causality. They argue, however, that their findings do broadly support the argument that faith school communities foster among their pupils the social capital necessary for higher attainment. They discuss this in terms of Catholic school effect and argue that their findings are consistent with the smaller positive effect found in relation to Catholic schools in the UK, rather than the larger effects associated with Catholic schools in the US. Given the current UK and US policies which encourage business and industry sponsorship for schools, it is interesting that this study found no positive effect on attainment in schools supported by business and trade unions. The model for involvement in Belgium may not be similar to the UK Academies and US charter schools programmes and so it is probably best not to read too much into this finding.

5.2.2 Netherlands

According to Glenn and de Groof (2002), the Netherlands has 'the most pluralistic school system in the world' (p. 349). It is not surprising, therefore, to find that much attention has been focussed on the Dutch system as a way of resolving the tensions of religious plurality in society and education. Non-government groups in the Netherlands have the right to establish schools, to give them a distinctive religious character, to organise them as they wish and to receive state funding. Walford (2001) has written about the influence of policy borrowing from the Netherlands on the campaign for funding by the new Christian schools.

Driessen (2002) has researched the relationship between pupils' majority or minority religious position in school and educational outcomes. This is set against the school effect argument that shared religious community and school creates social capital for pupils and improves performance. Driessen hypothesised that pupils in a position of religious dominance at school would perform

School effect may be weakened in a social context where religious communities have lost much of their importance.

better than pupils in a minority, but the data from 10,000 Dutch primary school pupils fails to confirm the hypothesis. The study used five effect measures to examine language and maths proficiency, social position, well-being and self-confidence. The analysis found no significant denominational effects and thus Driessen concludes that, 'taking into account the other attributes, the category of school which pupils attend clearly does not do anything for them' (p. 64). He attributes this to the increasing secularisation of society, arguing that as a process this weakens parental religious affiliation. This evidence seems to support the argument that school effect may be weakened in a social context where religious communities have lost much of their importance. Conversely, this may also demonstrate that there is a significant relationship between religious affiliation and denominational effect. In other words, schools with a Christian ethos are likely to have more impact when pupils have parents who are religiously committed and are also part of an active faith community. In relation to the context of policy borrowing between the UK and the Netherlands, these findings may cast doubt on the argument that schools can create social capital. Driessen (2002) found that family structures were much more significant in relation to pupil outcomes.

De Wolff, De Ruyter and Miedema (2003) examine the problem of the expression of 'Christian school identity' in the Netherlands. This expression is in widespread use in the Dutch literature on Christian schools and they argue that it belies a diverse picture. De Wolff, De Ruyter and Miedema researched concepts of identity and its consequences in three Protestant primary schools in the Netherlands. One school is described as a church-related Protestant orthodox school where all of the teachers and 98% of the pupils were practising church members. The other two schools were considered to be examples of more liberal Protestant schools with a more diverse religious background amongst the pupils; all of the teachers were Christians. This study does not primarily relate to the impact that schools with a Christian ethos in the Netherlands may have on pupils. Nevertheless, it provides important evidence about how identity, and therefore practices and outcomes, might be differently conceived by schools. The study compared the ideas and practices of teachers in the schools with each other and in relation to Dutch academic literature. These comparisons suggest that the interpretation of the 'religious' aspect of identity 'has the most influence on the aims and practices of a Christian school' (p. 207). Teachers at the orthodox Protestant schools were more likely to see themselves as role models for beliefs, morals and a lifestyle derived from their personal relationship with God. This corresponded with academic literature advocating Christian nurture as the central aim for Christian schools. De Wolff, De Ruyter and Miedema describe this as a one dimensional view of religious identity which centres on Christian faith as foundational and unchanging, and in which a Christian school is one that has a religious purpose. Within the literature they found an alternative concept of religious identity based on the view that schools are primarily pedagogical/educational institutions and should not be dominated by particular religious views or interests. De Wolff, De Ruyter and Miedema write that, 'in this view, the educational meaning and importance of basic Christian beliefs and values are not dependent on transmitting the Christian faith. Stimulating children towards beliefs and values like justice and servitude is considered to be of educational importance *per se*' (p. 216). The teachers in the two liberal Protestant schools thus conceptualised religious identity in terms of an ethical foundation in which Christian values were implicitly transmitted but in which religious plurality could be respected. This research emphasises once again that concepts of religious identity stem from particular views of knowledge and different theologies and can result in different institutional aims and practices.

> *Stimulating children towards beliefs and values like justice and servitude is considered to be of educational importance per se.*

5.2.3 Northern Ireland

Northern Ireland has been considered separately from England and Wales because of the very different political and religious context within which its system of education operates. All schools in Northern Ireland have a religious character. Historically, Protestant pupils attended Protestant schools and Catholic pupils attended Catholic schools, reflecting the sectarian social divide. This is why Northern Ireland is often cited as evidence in support of the argument that religious schools contribute to social segregation. Integrated schools for Catholic and Protestant pupils were first established by parents as part of the independent sector in the early 1980s. Educating pupils of different faiths together is regarded in the literature as a way of promoting social cohesion (Ouseley, 2001, Pennell *et al.*, 2007). This argument is often predicated on the basis of Troyna and Hatcher's (1992) 'contact hypothesis', which maintains that inter-personal contact across ethnic, race or religious lines promotes social cohesion (p. 24). Since 1989 Integrated schools have received state funding as long as they attract sufficient pupils to be viable.

> *Educating pupils of different faiths together is regarded in the literature as a way of promoting social cohesion.*

Donnelly (2000, 2008) has researched school ethos in Catholic and Integrated schools in Northern Ireland. Her research does not directly explore the impact of schools with a Christian ethos on pupils. The study has been included in the review because it raises important issues about how the concept of ethos has been regarded and researched in schools with a religious character. Donnelly (2000) argues that the way ethos has been defined in the literature is heavily dependent on research paradigms, or ways of knowing. She believes that researchers who take a positivist view are much more likely to 'view ethos as something which prescribes social reality' (p. 135). She argues that this type of research often takes a top down approach, treating ethos as a formal expression of an organisation's aims and objectives, embedded in mission statements and school policies. Donnelly argues that an anti-positivist perspective views ethos as something informal, emerging from social and group interactions. Donnelly researches school ethos from both these perspectives. She argues that tension is inherent in the gap between formal expressions of ethos and group interactions. These tensions arise between the values a school officially seeks to espouse, and the actual beliefs and values of individual school members.

Donnelly (2008) has also compared two types of Integrated schools and their approaches to promoting relationships between Catholic and Protestant pupils. Her work on Integrated schools provides an important perspective on how Christian ethos schools in a society divided on religious sectarian lines approach the issue of cultural difference. Based on qualitative interviews with teachers, governors and parents, the study found that although the way in which the schools promoted their ethos and image was different, there was little difference in the 'lived-reality' of the school as reported by research participants (p. 187). Donnelly found that the Integrated schools in her study tended not to refer to or to explore cultural or religious difference. She argues that this potentially silences 'school members who do wish to explore their own and other cultures' and concludes that this is more likely to impede than facilitate positive inter-community relationships (p. 187).

> *Tensions arise between the values a school officially seeks to espouse, and the actual beliefs and values of individual school members.*

Francis *et al.* (2006) replicated a study into the religious beliefs and values of both Catholic and Protestant pupils in Northern Irish schools originally carried out by Greer in 1984. Greer's study found significant and consistent differences in the religious profiles of the two denominational groups and the replication study confirmed these findings. Francis *et al.* 'examined the religious practices, religious beliefs, moral values, and views on the social role of the Church of 2,359 sixth-form pupils educated in the segregated school system of Northern Ireland' (p. 198). The significant differences between these two groups were reflected in five main ways:

1) Church attendance played a more important part in the Catholic community than in the Protestant community.
2) The Bible played a more important part in the Protestant community than in the Catholic community.
3) Protestants and Catholics nurtured different beliefs about the nature of God, with Catholics emphasising a loving image of God and Protestants a more judging image.
4) Protestants and Catholics inhabit different moral 'universes' (p. 199). The Protestants viewed God as being more against 'gambling, drunkenness, smoking, lying, stealing and sexual intercourse before marriage' (p. 199). The Catholics viewed God as being 'more against capital punishment, war, the use of nuclear weapons, colour prejudice and religious discrimination' (p. 199).
5) Protestants and Catholics had different views regarding the church's continuing influence over social life. The Catholic community was less sympathetic toward the Church's influence over morals and politics and more sympathetic toward its involvement in social issues (p. 199).

It should be noted that this study does not draw any conclusions about the effect of denominational schooling. In offering this kind of profile of religious beliefs, this study demonstrates that home and church communities are influential in the formation of Christian identity. Francis *et al.* also argue that the process of secularisation appears not to be so far advanced in Northern Ireland.

5.2.4 summary

In summary, the European studies demonstrate that positive Christian school effect is a powerful argument in defence of Christian schools in the European context. The right of religious groups to an education in keeping with their tradition and beliefs is supported in many European countries as a part of pluralist democracy. The research, however, does not agree on whether there is a significant Christian school effect on performance. Research done in the Netherlands could demonstrate no significant effect on performance, but research done in Belgium found a Catholic school effect size similar to that in the UK. Once again these studies have demonstrated that Christian ethos schooling is diverse. Research in the Netherlands suggests, however, that this diversity may be important in accounting for how individual schools understand their religious identity, distinctiveness and their aims and practices.

5.3 US

In the US, public schools are entirely secular; religious groups have the freedom to establish non-state schools and these are subject to conditions set by the individual states. As in the UK, considerable attention has been focussed on the higher attainment of pupils attending religious schools in the US. It has also been argued that schools with a religious character are better able to facilitate spiritual and moral development in their pupils. This is important because of a widespread perception in some quarters that the traditional religious and moral values of US society are under threat. It should be borne in mind that the political system in the US, in particular the influence of the new Christian right, is different than the UK and beyond the scope of this review. Nevertheless, there are similarities in the broader education policy agenda, particularly its focus upon declining moral and academic standards.

5.3.1 Catholic schools in the US

The largest system of religiously affiliated private schools in the US is Roman Catholic (Glenn and de Groof, 2002). Major work done by Bryk *et al.* (1993) has lent considerable weight to the argument that Catholic schools have a positive effect that cannot be accounted for in terms of social selection or pupil characteristics. Bryk *et al's* ten year project comprised in-depth studies of a small number of Catholic schools, 'statistical analysis of large data bases and an exploration of the philosophical and historical roots of catholic schools' (p. ix). The research found that ethnic minority pupils and pupils from more disadvantaged backgrounds performed better at Catholic schools than at public high schools. Drop out rates were lower in Catholic schools. The research attributes this academic success to a common core of academic work for all pupils; a supportive, communal style of organisation; decentralised governance; and an inspirational ideology. The study concluded that a philosophy of education strongly rooted in Catholic tradition, the promotion of community values, and a high regard for the development of the whole person (body, mind and spirit) promoted a greater social good. They argued that an integration of factors above and beyond pupil characteristics or organisational components accounted for the positive academic and community impact of Catholic schools in America. These integrated factors are commonly referred to in the wider literature as the Catholic school effect. Bryk *et al.* offered Catholic schools as a model for school improvement in the US.

5.3.2 comparative studies in the US

Blain and Revell (2002) explore two distinct approaches developed by the public school system and by religious private schools in Chicago as a response to concerns about declining morality and character development. Blain and Revell explain that 'in the absence of religious, spiritual or values education, many schools in the American public sector have adopted the Character Education approach' (p. 180). This aims to form in pupils individual traits of character valued by society and its traditions. Delivery of the Character Education programme is entirely decoupled from Religious Education. In contrast, in religious private schools, spiritual and moral development are firmly embedded in the Religious Education programme. (It should be noted that not all of the private religious schools included in their purposive sample were of Christian character; they visited Roman Catholic, Lutheran and Jewish schools.)

Blain and Revell visited a total of 21 elementary and high schools. In all schools they interviewed children, in small groups, from a variety of grades. They also interviewed teachers and either the Principal or Assistant Principal. Their findings cannot be generalised; rather they provide a rich description of the approaches developed by the schools visited. Blain and Revell found that all of the private schools taught religion as a discrete part of the curriculum and that teachers generally spoke about religion and faith with a passionate commitment. Consequently, these schools made no distinction between religious, moral, and spiritual education. In the public schools there was widespread suspicion of the value of teaching religion. Although nothing prohibits teachers from teaching about religion in the public school system, the majority of teachers felt that it would simply be too divisive and problematic to contemplate. All of the public schools distinguished between moral and character education. The Character Education programme was seen as being far less divisive than Religious Education approaches and, thus, more appropriate for multi-cultural and multi-ethnic pupil bodies. Blain and Revell conclude that, in both public and private school approaches, there is some danger that, unless educationalists are proactive in overcoming the obstacles, an open forum for teaching or discussing issues to do with religion will be lost' (p. 880).

Jeynes (2003) has carried out a number of large scale statistical reviews of the impact of religious schools on pupil attainment and learning behaviours. His research represents a significant evidence base for those who argue that Christian ethos schools promote higher attainment and develop social capital. Jeynes has analysed a large dataset pertaining to pupils in Grade 12. The National Educational Longitudinal Study (NELS) was a project sponsored by the US Department of Education's National Centre for Statistics. Jeynes' study draws on a population of 18,726 pupils who participated in the study in 1992. The study compares the learning habits of pupils attending Catholic, evangelical and other religious schools with those not attending religious schools. In the first analyses Jeynes tested variables derived from specific areas which researchers believe may explain the achievement gap between pupils. These areas comprise:

> *Unless educationalists are proactive in overcoming the obstacles, an open forum for teaching or discussing issues to do with religion will be lost.*

1) Handing work in on time more regularly.
2) Less absenteeism.
3) Taking harder courses.
4) Maintaining a higher level of diligence.
5) Demonstrating better work habits.
6) Paying more attention in school.
7) Doing more work than expected.
8) Participating in class.
9) Being prepared for class.

In a second analysis, Jeynes tested if these variables were indeed related to academic achievement and the extent to which this was the case. Finally, a further analysis was done to determine if there were differences in the learning habits and achievement between Catholic and non-Catholic religious pupils. Jeynes also analysed the degree to which family religiosity may have affected academic orientation.

The results of this analysis indicate that 'religious school pupils outperform non-religious school pupils in five of the nine categories' (p. 145). These five categories comprised: i) handing work in on time, ii) taking harder courses, iii) greater diligence, iv) better work habits and v) paying more attention in school. Jeynes points out that, 'the two categories in which religious school pupils outperform their non-religious counterparts the most, diligence and taking harder courses, were the two categories most strongly related to performing well on achievement tests' (p. 145). He argues that greater diligence and taking harder courses could be the result of two possibilities. First, religious schools may instil a better work ethic in pupils, or second, pupils attending religious school may already have a good work ethic, perhaps explained by the religiosity of their family. Jeynes' analysis is unable to determine which of these is the case.

Jeynes also compared the results of Catholic pupils with non-Catholic religious pupils, usually evangelical pupils. He found that, although Catholic pupils demonstrated greater diligence, the other religious pupils had an advantage in four work habits: i) a more demanding school programme, ii) paying attention in class, iii) handing work in on time and iv) participating in class. Jeynes points out the somewhat surprising finding that participating in class was negatively correlated with academic achievement. This study cannot demonstrate that the learning behaviours of pupils attending religious schools were directly caused by school effect. Jeynes argues, however, that the positive findings are unlikely to be accidental and concludes that school must influence learning habits.

> *Religious school advantage can be greater at secondary levels.*

Jeynes (2003) has argued that educators in the US concerned about pupil outcomes should look to religious schools as a model. He conducted a meta-analysis of the research examining the influence of religious schools versus public schools over the last twenty years (Jeynes, 2004). The analysis of 56 studies included research done in elementary and secondary schools. When the elementary and secondary research was combined, no statistically significant differences were demonstrated. The analysis did find that in the early studies, religious schools demonstrated an advantage at elementary level; in the more recent studies they demonstrated an advantage at secondary level. This is consistent with findings from earlier research which demonstrated that religious school advantage can be greater at secondary levels (Coleman *et al.*, 1982, Jeynes, 2003). Jeynes writes that, 'the results indicate that the influence of religious schools versus public schools on pupil educational outcomes has remained quite consistent over time' (p. 197).

The evidence from this meta-analysis of studies supports the argument that religious schools improve educational outcomes. It also suggests that sociological and economic factors do not 'dilute the effect'; in other words, that something other than social selection and pupil characteristics explains pupil performance. What the meta-analysis cannot do, however, is explain the causes of school effect or the nature of its relationship to higher pupil attainment.

The review found a study in the US which did attempt to research the nature of school effect and disentangle the impact of parents' and peer-group religiosity (i.e. the active religious life of the peer group and parents). Using data from the National Survey of Youth and Religion (NSYR), Uecker (2008) compared the religious lives of pupils in five different types of school: i) Catholic, ii) Protestant, iii) public, iv) home schooled and v) secular private schools. The research tested three mechanisms through which schooling strategies may influence religiosity: i) friendship networks, ii) network closure (this refers to the membership of close-knit religious communities which act to reinforce particular religious values) and iii) adult mentors. Uecker found that the religiosity of parents had a significant role in the religious involvement of adolescents and that this was not mediated by school type. The study found that parents and peers had a much greater influence than schooling over all aspects of pupils' religious lives. Taking into account the religiosity of parents and friends as well as other mediating variables, Uecker did find that the pupils attending Protestant schools were more likely to exhibit a more active private religious life. He suggests that immersion in Protestant religious culture that places a premium on personal religiosity may explain this. On church-related activities such as attending church or Sunday school, no difference was found between pupils attending Catholic and Protestant schools and pupils attending the other categories of school. Although Uecker's research was unable to deal adequately with the problem of selection due to the nature of the NSYR data, it does seem to suggest that schools of different types may impact pupil religiosity in different ways. Uecker recommends that more research be done to determine the long term impact of schooling strategies on the religiosity of pupils.

5.3.3 summary

These examples of research into the impact of schools with a Christian ethos in the US demonstrate a similar preoccupation with the standards and school effectiveness debate, and the challenge to traditional moral and spiritual education raised by modern pluralist society. Some inroads have been made in accounting for school effect and the impact of different types of Christian ethos school. More research is needed to account for the nature of religious school effect and to determine whether it accounts for higher pupil attainment.

5.4 summary of the international research perspective

The examples of international research reviewed in this chapter clearly do not constitute a global picture. What is interesting is that, despite diverse methodologies, school types and national contexts, common research issues and questions do emerge, reflecting those identified in the UK research. The first of these concerns the concept of Christian school identity and distinctiveness, particularly in response to post-modern paradigms of knowledge, and the loss of authority that traditional religious institutions have experienced in contemporary society. According to the literature, some researchers and some schools in Australasia, Europe and the US have responded to this challenge by reasserting traditional concepts of religious beliefs, structure and practice as a counter to spiritual and moral decline. This approach is often associated with the SESI research paradigm, defending the effectiveness of schools with a Christian ethos on the grounds of strong organisational culture and leadership. There were fewer examples in the literature of research studies, or of schools, beginning to deal with the problems of religious identity, moral and spiritual development in the light of pupils' contemporary experience, but there were some. The second common theme was the relationship between religiosity and the impact of schools. The research seemed to suggest that religiosity of teachers, pupils and parents may have an impact on a wide range of factors, from pedagogy, to attainment, to embedding a good work ethic. As with the UK research, this focus seems to indicate that religiosity is an important predictor of beliefs and values and is likely to be relevant in any account of school effect. A third common research focus was the relationship between religious schools and pupil attainment and learning behaviours. Whilst some of the European research is contradictory, broadly the evidence seems to support the UK finding that schools with a Christian ethos have a positive impact on achievement.

chapter 5 - references

1. See http://www.argentisys.com.
2. TIMSS is a worldwide research project collecting international data every four years to provide data about trends in mathematics and science achievement over time (see timss.bc.edu/).

conclusions and recommendations for future research

When cartographers drew up the earliest maps of the New World they worked from the coastal charts and diagrams of the first explorers. The results were detailed maps of narrow strips of land stretching along coastlines and on either side of the rivers. We are now, of course, familiar with the vast stretches that lay beyond these markers and were left blank, or vaguely sketched, in the originals. This is a good analogy of where we are when it comes to mapping the field of current Christian education research. We are using the work of the early explorers.

The aim of this review was to summarise and evaluate what the current research says about the impact of schools with a Christian ethos upon the attainment, beliefs, attitudes, behaviours and spirituality of pupils. What has become clear is that the research does not present one clear picture. There is danger in 'picking and mixing' studies which use different research methodologies and are rooted in different assumptions about the nature of Christian distinctiveness, and hence, the purpose and impact of schools with a Christian ethos. At the risk of pushing an analogy too far, Christopher Columbus was mistaken when he thought he had reached India.

6.1 conclusions and observations

In conclusion, the review found the following positive evidence about the impact of schools with a Christian ethos. In the context of the UK, this comprises three main findings:

1) Pupils at church-maintained schools and independent Christian schools showed a more positive attitude towards religion and better spiritual health than pupils in other schools.

2) In terms of attainment, the evidence supported the widespread perception that pupils at maintained church schools achieve more highly and make better progress than pupils at non-denominational schools. The research suggested that prior attainment and pupil characteristics do not completely account for this. There is some 'school effect'.

3) The research suggests that religious affiliation may be a significant predictor of both individual behaviour and positive attitude towards religion.

These findings were further substantiated by the small sample of international research studies that were reviewed. The international research shared a number of commonalities with the UK research in terms of focus (see chapter 5 section 4), and the evidence pointed to similar conclusions. Evidence from the international research appeared to substantiate the following conclusions:

> *Religious affiliation may be a significant predictor of both individual behaviour and positive attitude towards religion.*

1) Religiosity is a significant predictor of behaviour and attitudes.

2) Pupils at schools with a Christian ethos attain more highly than pupils at non-religious schools (see especially US research).

3) Pupils at schools with a Christian ethos exhibit more of the learning habits associated with better achievement than pupils at non-religious schools (see especially US research).

In addition, ten key conclusions concerning the characteristics of the research reviewed may be drawn:

1) Very little research has been carried out in the last ten years into the impact of schools with a Christian ethos on the attainment, beliefs, attitudes, behaviour and spiritual development of pupils.

2) Most of the research that has been carried out attempts to measure the impact of schools with a Christian ethos on (a) attainment and (b) attitudes towards religion, particularly Christianity.

3) There does not appear to be a common language amongst researchers or research participants for talking about values, character development, spirituality or ethos; nor are there agreed definitions for these concepts.

4) There is a particular lack of clarity regarding the concept of spirituality.

5) There is a lack of consensus regarding the purpose of, and contribution to be made by, Christian distinctiveness in education.

6) The research does not appear to be able to disentangle the impact of home, school and church on pupils' attainment, beliefs, attitudes, behaviour and spiritual development.

7) Although the concept of 'school effect' is a key idea in a lot of the research into the impact of schools with a Christian ethos, it is unclear what this means; very little in-depth work has been done in an attempt to account for 'school effect'.

8) It is not possible to draw conclusions about the differing impact of the different types of Christian ethos school.

9) Research into schools with a Christian ethos is often motivated by the need to justify their existence and, in particular, their government funding.

10) The research is shaped by different research paradigms with their attendant assumptions about ways of knowing, theology and research methodology. This, in turn, shapes the view of Christian distinctiveness and the understanding of Christian ethos embedded in each research project.

6.1.1 Discussion

The lack of research into schools with a Christian ethos is disappointing because it means it is hard to say much about their impact. From a UK perspective, this is particularly of concern, given the focus that there has been on schools with a Christian ethos among policy makers and considering the high profile debate regarding the contribution of faith schools to social cohesion. The bias in the research towards measuring the impact of schools with a Christian ethos on attainment reflects global shifts in education policy. An increasing preoccupation with academic standards and individual pupil performance frames the context within which all schools operate and are judged to be successful. In England and Wales, maintained schools with a Christian ethos have been directly co-opted into this agenda because of the perception that they raise standards and that Christian character formation will promote diligence, hard-work and attainment.

The main factors that make it difficult to reach definitive conclusions on the impact of Christian ethos schools are:

- The *justification* for the existence of Christian ethos schools, in particular their receipt of state funding, is one key theme that influences the research agenda across the diversity of school type and methodologies. (For discussion from a Christian perspective on this see, for example, Cooling, 2007, Smith, 2000, Pike, 2004.) One of the most significant concepts discussed is individual rational autonomy. Dwyer (1998), Hand (2003, 2001) and Mason (2003, 2005), to name but a few, have argued cogently that confessional education does not allow children to make individual rational autonomous choices about religious belief. They regard this as compromising a basic human right. Equally cogently, educational philosophers such as Thiessen (1993) and Pring (2005) argue that faith is constitutive of being human. It is their argument that confessional education or participation in a faith tradition is actually integral to attaining individual autonomy.

Thiessen advocates the concept of 'normal autonomy' being fully compatible with participation in a faith community. This debate is important, because its existence creates nervousness and anxiety amongst researchers, policy makers and school leaders concerning the justification for schools with a distinctively Christian ethos. No one wants to be accused of indoctrination.

- A related point is that the evidence from this research review suggests that headteachers at Christian ethos schools were influenced in their perceptions by the criticism that their schools did not promote social cohesion. Some headteachers, therefore, played down the importance of distinctive Christian teaching and church doctrines, which had historically defined concepts such as spirituality in accordance with Christian tradition. By contrast, some headteachers responded to this criticism by reinforcing traditional definitions. Others still could not see the relevance of Christian ethos to the core work of the school. When the same terms are used in the research but with different underpinning meanings and valuations, the result is a lack of clarity.

> *Researchers and schools lack a shared language with which to conceptualise and discuss the nature, purpose and impact of distinctively Christian education.*

- A key factor is that researchers and schools lack a shared language with which to conceptualise and discuss the nature, purpose and impact of distinctively Christian education. This is evidenced by the range of proxies found within the studies and the variety of research carried out. It is further complicated by a lack of agreed definitions for such terms as 'spirituality' and 'Christian ethos'. Education policy has focussed on academic and social capital outcomes, and largely ignored the philosophical underpinnings of the subject curriculum. This means that, until recently, questions have not been systematically asked by policy makers, researchers and research participants about the nature of values and character education embedded within the different views of Christian distinctiveness. The focus on attainment and on measuring impact has led research in the direction of statistical analysis of school outputs, particularly standards of academic achievement. Studies that investigate the relationships between the desired Christian ethos, and the school's processes and structures and their impact on pupils, are less common.

- The lack of clarity found at a number of levels within the research is attributable, at least in part, to the range of research paradigms employed, with their attendant different assumptions about ways of knowing and the nature of evidence. This has implications for the way that researchers define and use significant concepts, for example, spirituality. In consequence, researchers may well be asking different questions in relation to the impact of schools with a Christian ethos predicated on particular views of pedagogy, culture and even theology. Research into the spiritual impact of schools with a Christian ethos was a key example of this within the literature reviewed. For example, Erricker (2007) positions himself firmly within a post-modern paradigm, arguing that spirituality is highly individual and that pupils must simply be equipped to explore their own sense of wonder, mystery and the transcendent. In other words the journey is more significant than the arrival at a destination, spirituality cannot be 'measured', and judgements may not be imposed as to what constitutes appropriate or inappropriate forms of spiritual development. Hay (2006) is convinced that the spiritual is part of our fundamental biology and argues that although we may be socialised into repressing this aspect of our personhood, particularly in adolescence, spirituality is a significant way in which we explore and understand the world.

> *Although we may be socialised into repressing this aspect of our personhood, spirituality is a significant way in which we explore and understand the world.*

Similarly Francis and Robbins (2005) understand attitudes towards religion to be powerful predictors of individual difference. They thus apply Fisher *et al's* (2000) model of spiritual health within a research paradigm that assumes spirituality is relational, rather than individual, that it can be measured, and that pupils may exhibit 'better' or 'worse' spiritual health. These examples demonstrate that when researchers use the term 'spirituality', they are applying very different understandings of the concept derived from conflicting research paradigms.

- At the most fundamental level the review reveals that there is little, if any, consensus around what constitutes a school with a Christian ethos. Badley *et al.* (1998) wrestle with the issue of how one even identifies a 'Christian' school. They discuss whether there is such a thing as a continuum of schools from 'anti- or non-Christian on one end, to intensely and thoroughly Christian on the other' (p. 40). The review found that there is disagreement over what constitutes appropriate aims for schools with a Christian ethos in current Western society. Two clear examples of this were found in the literature:

    1) Some researchers argue passionately that schools with a Christian ethos are largely failing to address the declining acceptance of church authority and traditional understandings of religious truth among teachers and pupils. They argue that schools need to reflect on their traditional ways of thinking about

knowledge and religious truth, to reflect changes in how contemporary society defines concepts such as spirituality (see for example McLaughlin, 2005, Street, 2007, Jelfs, 2008).

2) Other researchers believe passionately that schools with a Christian ethos offer a distinctive answer to the moral and religious breakdown in current society. They argue that character education and morality anchored in traditional understandings of Christian beliefs can raise aspirations and develop a deeper sense of values and personhood (see for example Ap Sion *et al.*, 2007, Francis *et al.*, in press, Pike, 2009).

These different views of Christian distinctiveness have implications for the research questions being explored and the methodologies employed in the literature. The review found that researchers who interpreted distinctiveness in terms of nurture and identity formation within the Christian community, are more likely to identify a Christian school in terms of its formal religious practices and Religious Education. They are more likely to measure impact in terms of pupils' attitudes towards religion. Researchers with a more holistic view of Christian distinctiveness are more likely to emphasise the implicit ways in which schools with a Christian ethos can promote shared values and support pupils' own faith or non-faith traditions. They are more likely to measure impact in terms of the development of personal spirituality or spiritual health. The review found that this lack of consensus is often obscured in the literature because the studies are not explicit about the view of Christian distinctiveness which underpins the research.

The research makes little attempt to disentangle the impact of church, home and school on pupils.

- Despite the persistence in the literature of a concept of 'school effect', the research makes little attempt to disentangle the impact of church, home and school on pupils. Major studies into the attitudes of pupils attending denominational schools do not collect data on the religious background of pupils. This makes it very difficult to report specifically on the impact of schools with a Christian ethos or their religious composition. The research seems to suggest that family and peer group, not necessarily school peer group, may be more influential in the development of beliefs, attitudes, behaviour and spiritual development than teachers or school ethos. Even this remains unclear simply because so little work has been done in this area.

- Similarly, much of the research into the impact on pupils of schools with a Christian ethos, aggregates data collected from diverse institutions. School types such as 'Church of England' or 'Independent' are not homogenous categories. This would seem to make it even more important to be able to differentiate within the research between different types of schools with a Christian ethos, and their impact on the beliefs, attitudes, behaviour and spiritual development of pupils. In order to ascertain what impact a school with a Christian ethos is having on pupils, a clear understanding of what is understood by being distinctively Christian is required.

6.1.2 Summary

In summary, from the literature reviewed we cannot draw a comprehensive map of the field. This is not just because little research has been done, but because the research reflects different agendas and assumptions that are not always compatible. Just as different maps might chart topography or population density as opposed to routes of navigation, so researchers are interested in different aspects of Christian ethos schools and their impact. This report concludes that the desire to justify the existence of schools with a Christian ethos, together with a broader policy context emphasising pupil attainment, has led to a focus in the literature on measuring impact in terms of pupil academic performance. The report also concludes that the presence of different research paradigms in the literature and different conceptions of Christian distinctiveness result in a lack of clarity around such concepts as values, ethos and spirituality. This is further complicated by the ways in which traditional religious definitions of spirituality, values and morality are being challenged by new global trends. When these terms occur in the literature they can mean very different things, depending on the research paradigm and the researchers' assumptions about ways of knowing or their concepts of religious truth. Finally, the report concludes that the literature is unable to account for school effect or report fully on its impact. Not enough is known about the relationships between different conceptions of Christian distinctiveness, school type and the additional influences of home and church on pupils' beliefs, attitudes, behaviour and spiritual development.

6.2 Recommendations for future research

The review of the literature has demonstrated that this is an underdeveloped research field. This means that there are potentially many areas in which future research could profitably be carried out. In shaping the recommendations made in this report, the following six key points from the review have been judged to be of particular significance:

1) The lack of clarity on the part of both researchers and schools as to what is meant by a school with a Christian ethos has made it difficult to draw conclusions as to the impact of these schools. This lack of clarity may account for the lack of confidence that appears to exist on the part of some headteachers in the legitimacy of a distinctive Christian ethos.

2) Similarly, the lack of clarity on what is meant by the term 'impact' makes the drawing of conclusions difficult, as different research reports may be reporting on fundamentally different things.

3) The diversity of the schools studied and of the research paradigms used made it difficult to reach secure conclusions. Many studies appeared to treat schools as though they were all the same when there was probably a diversity of policies and practices represented within the group.

4) Although there probably is some school effect, it has been difficult to distinguish this from the impact that the home and family might have.

5) The external pressure from governmental and parental concern with academic standards has meant that much of the research has focussed on studying the impact of schools with a Christian ethos on attainment, rather than their spiritual impact.

6) There were certain research approaches that seemed to have particular potential for tracking the impact of the Christian ethos of the school. They were those that examined how planned interventions in one school impacted on pupils. Examples were Deakin Crick (2002), Collier & Dowson (2007) and, to a degree, Green (forthcoming). These studies indicate that it is possible to devise measures of impact in response to a planned intervention and thereby create a controlled research situation. Indeed the paper by Chaney (2008), although not a peer-reviewed research study, provided tantalising hints as to some of the possibilities.

6.2.1 A new framework for future research

This report proposes a framework for future research which takes account of the six key points described in section 6.2 above. The fact that different understandings of knowing and different worldviews have implications for the understanding of Christian distinctiveness adopted is thought to be particularly significant. In the proposed framework (see figure 1), four different categories of Christian ethos schools are identified. These categories were drawn from the literature and from the review group's knowledge of the field. The four categories are meant to represent four main views of the desired impact of schools with a distinctive Christian ethos. They are:

1) The nurture of identity within the context of a Christian school community.

2) The promotion of the well-being and spirituality of all pupils.

3) The formation of character and production of positive citizens (a social capital model).

4) The enhancement of pupils' academic performance.

Different worldviews have implications for the understanding of Christian distinctiveness adopted.

These are not necessarily mutually exclusive categories; one school may take its main identity from one of them, but see itself as having an impact on another. For example, a school in category one may have as its goal the nurture of Christian faith, but see itself as contributing to the character development of all pupils, irrespective of their own faith.

1) Category one comprises schools that understand their distinctiveness in the context of the Christian community and mission. They would be concerned about the extent to which Christian distinctiveness at the school impacts pupils' own identity. Catholic schools are a clear example of category one, as are CST linked schools. Indeed *The Way Ahead* report (Dearing, 2001), arguably places all Church of England schools (certainly aided schools) in this category, in its affirmation that, 'Church schools stand at the centre of the Church's mission to the nation' (page 1).

2) Category two conceptualizes Christian distinctiveness in terms of the well-being and spiritual development of the whole child, regardless of their membership of the Christian faith community. The presence of diverse ethnic and religious traditions in society, and within the school community, can lead to a greater emphasis on shared values and less explicitly Christian instruction within this category. This would be exemplified by some Church of England schools which emphasize their responsibility to educate all of the children in the locality regardless of whether they practise a Christian faith. In *The Way Ahead* report (Dearing, 2001) this is described as the service function of church schools to the whole community.

3) Category three offers a view of distinctiveness in which Christianity forms a moral and ethical framework for character formation and promoting civic values. In England this would be exemplified by many traditional private schools that have a Christian foundation and, probably, the ESF schools. This focus often evokes a sense of England's past cultural and civic sensibilities and would reflect some of the discussions about 'British-ness'.

4) Finally, category four exemplifies the way in which Christian distinctiveness has been conceptualised in relation to pupil performance. Christian distinctiveness is seen as contributing to the promotion of learning habits and social development which are integral to higher academic achievement.

figure 1: New framework for research

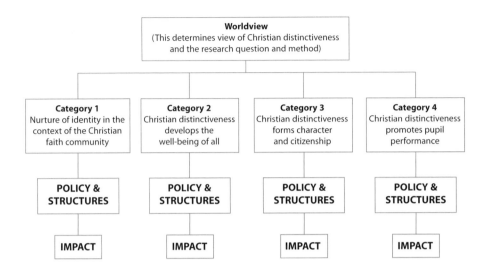

6.2.2 future research: a way forward

The review group's view was that category one schools should be the focus of any future research, given the growing emphasis within the Christian churches on the relationship between Christian distinctiveness, student identity and the notion that schools are central to the *mission of the Church*. Many of the new schools and academies being set up in England aspire to be in this category. These institutions will aim to nurture faith, but will also have a strong emphasis on the contribution that education in schools with a Christian ethos makes to the promotion of well-being, character formation, spiritual development, citizenship and high attainment of all pupils, irrespective of their own faith. Research on category one schools will therefore contribute to our knowledge and understanding of the likely impact of schools in the other three categories.

Key Question: How can future research contribute to our understanding of the impact on pupils' attainment, beliefs, attitudes, behaviour and spiritual development of schools with a Christian ethos, by which we mean schools that understand Christian distinctiveness in education in terms of *fulfilling the mission of the Church?*

With respect to the framework this key question would necessitate research activity at three levels:

1) At the level of worldview, to clarify the meaning of the language and concepts being taken as normative. In particular, this would entail developing a clear understanding of the nature and purpose of a category one, Christian ethos school. Only schools which clearly fell within the parameters thereby established should be studied.

2) At the level of structure and processes, to clarify how the aspirations to be a Christian ethos school are worked out in practice within the school.

3) At the level of impact, to ascertain what difference is being made to pupils through attendance at a Christian ethos school.

Our conclusion is that the most fruitful future research will be studies that investigate the impact of planned interventions made in individual schools that are clearly category one schools. By planned interventions, we mean examples of policies, structures and practices that are implemented with the intention of promoting the aims of the school, as defined through the process of clarifying the worldview being assumed and where their impact can be measured.

From this research, a typology could be created to enable the analysis of data collected from similar types of school, for example church voluntary aided schools or Academies with Christian sponsors. Impact could then be reported for category one schools as a whole.

6.2.3 Summary

The report recommends that future research be carried out at the level of worldview and school structure and processes, *as well as* at the level of impact on pupils, so as to build a full picture of the influence and impact on pupils of schools with a Christian ethos. In particular, it is recommended that research studies in individual schools that seek to discern the impact of designed interventions will be particularly fruitful.

The type of research recommended utilises well-established methodologies in educational research. It necessitates qualitative and quantitative research at institutional level and across institutions. This type of research, together with careful theory building, is needed, if any kind of comprehensive evidence-base for the impact of schools with a Christian ethos on pupils' attainment, beliefs, attitudes, behaviour and spiritual development is to be offered.

references

Acheson, B. (2003) Choruses from the rock: Developing SQ, Chaplaincy Papers. [Online] Bristol: Clifton College. Available from: < http://www.bloxhamproject.org.uk/archive.htm > (Accessed 9 May, 2009).

Adams, A. (2004) Ruminations of faith in leadership: Reflections on leadership from a Bloxham Project Day at Worth School. [Online] Bloxham: Bloxham Project. Available from: < http://www.bloxhamproject.org.uk/archive.htm > (Accessed 9 May, 2009).

Allder, M. (1993) The meaning of 'school ethos'. *Westminster Studies in Education,* 16, pp. 59-69.

Ap Sion, T., Francis, L. J. & Baker, S. (2007) Experiencing education in the new Christian schools in the United Kingdom: Listening to the male graduates. *Journal of Beliefs and Values,* 28, (1), pp. 1-15.

Arthur, J. (2003) *Education with character.* London: Routledge.

Arthur, J. (2009) Church of England schools research: Values and character dispositions of 14-16 year olds. Canterbury: National Institute for Christian Education Research.

Arthur, J., Deakin Crick, R., Samuel, E., Wilson, K. & McGettrick, B. (2006) Character education: The formation of virtues and dispositions in 16-19 year olds with particular reference to the religious and spiritual. Canterbury & Bristol: Canterbury Christ Church University and the University of Bristol.

Arthur, J. & Godfrey, R. (2005) Statistical survey of the attainment and achievement of pupils in Church of England schools. Canterbury: National Institute for Christian Education Research.

Badley, K. (1998) Identifying Christian schools: How do you tell when you've found one? *Journal of Education & Christian Belief,* 2, (1) pp. 39-51.

Baker, S. & Freeman, D. (2005) *The love of God in the classroom.* Ross-shire: Christian Focus.

Berkely, R. (2008) The right to divide. Runnymede: The Runnymede Trust.

Blain, M. & Revell, L. (2002) Patterns of spiritual and moral development in religious and public schools in Chicago. *Journal of Beliefs & Values,* 23, (2), pp. 179-189.

The Bloxham Project (2007) The spiritual dimension of school leadership. Cuddesdon, Oxford: The Bloxham Project, Ripon College.

The Bloxham Project (2008) Youth spirituality: Where are we exactly? Project Papers 39. Cuddesdon, Oxford: The Bloxham Project, Ripon College.

Brown, A. (2003) Church of England schools: Politics, power and identity. *British Journal of Religious Education,* 52, (2), pp. 103-115.

Bryk, A., Lee, V. & Holland, P. (1993) *Catholic schools and the common good.* Cambridge, MA: Harvard University Press.

Chaney, M. (2008) Reflections on some governance challenges. Australia: Address given at the Australian Anglican Schools Network Annual Conference in Perth, 22 August 2008.

Coleman, J. S., Hoffer, T. & Kilgore, S. (1982) *High school achievement: Public, Catholic and private schools compared.* New York: Basic Books.

Collier, J. & Dowson, M. (2007) Applying an action research approach to improving the quality of Christian education – one school's experience. *Journal of Christian Education,* 50, (1), pp. 27-36.

Colson, I. (2004) 'Their churches are at home': The communication and definition of values in four aided Church of England secondary schools. *British Journal of Religious Education,* 26, (1), pp. 73-84.

Cooling, T. (2007) The challenge of passionate religious commitment for school education in a world of religious diversity: reflections on evangelical Christianity and humanism. *Journal of Education & Christian Belief,* 11, (1), pp. 23-34.

Curran, M. & Francis, L. J. (1996) Measuring 'Catholic identity' among pupils in Catholic secondary schools. In L. J. Francis, W. R. Kay, and W. S. Campbell (eds) *Research into Religious Education.* Leominster: Gracewing, pp. 383-391.

Curtis, A. (2009) Academies and school diversity. *Management in Education,* 23, (3), pp.113-117.

Davies, G. (2007) Spiritual development in church schools: a survey of Welsh head teachers' perceptions. *International Journal of Children's Spirituality,* 12, (3), pp. 307-324.

Davies, G. & Francis, L. J. (2007) Three approaches to Religious Education at Key Stages One and Two in Wales: How different are church schools? *Journal of Beliefs & Values,* 28, (2), pp. 163-182.

DCSF (2007) *Faith in the system: The role of schools with a religious character in English education and society.* London: DCSF Publications.

De Wolff, A. J. C., De Ruyter, D. J. & Miedema, S. (2003) Being a Christian school in the Netherlands: An analysis of 'identity' conceptions and their practical implications. *Journal of Beliefs and Values,* 24, (2), pp. 207-217.

Deakin, R. (1989) *The new Christian schools.* Bristol: The Regius Press Ltd on behalf of The Christian Schools Trust.

Deakin Crick, R. (2002) Integrating faith and learning: An empirical case study from a Church of England secondary school. *Whitefield Briefing,* 7.

Deakin Crick, R., Broadfoot, P. & Claxton, G. (2004) Developing an effective lifelong learning inventory: The ELLI Project. *Assessment in Education Principles Policy and Practice,* 11, (3), pp. 247-272.

Dearing, R. (2001) *The Way Ahead: Church of England schools in the new millennium. [Online].* The National Society for promoting Religious Education. Available from: < http://www.natsoc.org.uk/schools/the_way_ahead/ > (Accessed 9 May, 2009).

DfES (2005) *Academies: Schools to make a difference,* Nottingham: DfES Publications.

Dixon, R. (2004) Acceptance of key Catholic beliefs and moral teachings by Generation X Mass attenders. *The Australasian Catholic Record,* 81.

Donnelly, C. (2000) In pursuit of school ethos. *British Journal of Educational Studies,* 48, (2), pp. 134-154.

Donnelly, C. (2008) The Integrated School in a Conflict Society: A comparative analysis of two integrated primary schools in Northern Ireland. *Cambridge Journal of Education,* 38, (2), pp. 187-198.

Driessen, G. W. J. M. (2002) The effect of religious groups' dominance in classrooms on cognitive and non-cognitive educational outcomes. *International Journal of Education and Religion,* 3, (1), pp. 46-68.

Dwyer, J. (1998) *Religious schools versus children's rights.* Ithaca, New York: Cornell University Press.

Emmanuel Schools Foundation (2007) *Mission statement and our Core Values. Personal Study File 2006-2007.* Gateshead: Emmanuel City Technology College.

Erricker, C. (2007) Children's spirituality and postmodern faith. *International Journal of Children's Spirituality,* 12, (1) pp. 51-60.

Fisher, J. W. (1999) Helps to fostering students' spiritual health. *International Journal of Children's Spirituality,* 4, (1), pp. 29-49.

Fisher, J. W. (2004) Feeling good, living life: A spiritual health measure for young children. *Journal of Beliefs & Values,* 25, (3), pp. 307-315.

Fisher, J. W. (2006) Using secondary students' views about influences on their spiritual well-being to inform pastoral care. *International Journal of Children's Spirituality,* 11, (3), pp. 347-356.

Fisher, J. W. (2008) Impacting teachers' and students' spiritual well-being. *Journal of Beliefs & Values,* 29, (3), pp. 253-261.

Fisher, J. W., Francis, L. J. & Johnson, P. (2000) Assessing spiritual health via four domains of well-being: The SH4DI. *Pastoral Psychology,* 49, (2), pp. 229-243.

Flynn, M. & Mok, M. (2000) Catholic schools 2000: A longitudinal study of Year 12 students in Catholic schools 1972–1982–1990–1998. Sydney: Catholic Education Commission, NSW.

Francis, L. J. (1982) *Youth in Transit: A profile of 16-25 year-*olds. Aldershot: Gower.

Francis, L. J. (1984a) *Teenagers and the church: A profile of church-going youth in the 1980s.* London: Collins Liturgical Publications.

Francis, L. J. (1984b) *Young and Unemployed.* Tunbridge Wells: Costello.

Francis, L. J. (2001) *The values debate: A voice from the pupils.* London: Woburn Press.

Francis, L. J. (2002) Catholic schools and Catholic values: A study of moral and religious values among 13-15 year old pupils attending non-denominational and Catholic schools in England and Wales. *International Journal of Education and Religion,* 3, (1), pp. 69-84.

Francis, L. J. (2005) Independent Christian schools and pupil values: An empirical investigation among 13-15 year old boys. *British Journal of Religious Education, 27*, (2), pp. 127-141.

Francis, L. J. (in press) Comparative empirical research in religion: Conceptual and operational challenges within empirical theology. In L.J. Francis, M. Robbins & J. Astley (eds) *Empirical theology in texts and tables: Qualitative, quantitative and comparative perspectives.* Leiden: Brill.

Francis, L. J., Ap Sion, T. & Baker, S. (in press) The theological case for Christian schools in England and Wales: A qualitative perspective listening to female alumnae. In L.J. Francis, M. Robbins & J. Astley (eds.) *Empirical theology in texts and tables: Qualitative, quantitative and comparison perspectives.* Leiden: Brill.

Francis, L. J. & Jewell, A. (1992) Shaping adolescent attitude towards the church: comparison between Church of England and county secondary schools. *Evaluation and research in education, 6*, pp. 13-21.

Francis, L. J. & Kay, W. K. (1995) *Teenage religion and values.* Leominster: Gracewing.

Francis, L. J., Robbins, M., Barnes, P. & Lewis, C. A. (2006) Religiously affiliated schools in Northern Ireland: The persistence of denominational differences in pupils' religious and moral values. *Journal of Empirical Theology, 19*, (2), pp.182-202.

Francis, L. J. & Robbins, M. (2005) *Urban hope and spiritual health: The adolescent voice.* Peterborough: Epworth.

Gay, B. (2000) Fostering spiritual development through the religious dimension of schools: The report of a pilot study in 17 independent schools. *International Journal of Children's Spirituality, 5*, (1), pp. 61-74.

Gibbons, S. & Silva, O. (2006) Faith primary schools: Better schools or better pupils? [Online]. Centre for the Economics of Education, LSE. Available from: <
http://www.lse.ac.uk/collections/pressAndInformationOffice
/newsAndEvents//archives/2006/FaithPrimarySchools.htm > (Accessed 9 May, 2009).

Gill, R. (1999) *Churchgoing and Christian ethics.* Cambridge: Cambridge University Press.

Glenn, C. & De Groof, J. (2002) *Finding the right balance: Freedom, autonomy and accountability in education.* Utrecht: Lemma.

Godfrey, R. (2009) Faith schools and socio-economic deprivation: a statistical enquiry. Canterbury: National Institute for Christian Education Research.

Godfrey, R. & Morris, A. (2008) Explaining high attainment in faith schools: The impact of Religious Education and other examinations on pupils' GCSE points scores. *British Journal of Religious Education, 30*, (3), pp. 211-222.

Grace, G. (2002) *Catholic schools: Mission, markets and morality.* London: RoutledgeFalmer.

Grace, G. (2003a) Educational studies and faith-based schooling; moving from prejudice to evidence-based argument. *British Journal of Educational Studies, 52* (2), pp.149-167.

Grace, G. (2003b) First and foremost the church offers its educational service to the poor: Class, inequality, and Catholic schooling in contemporary contexts. *International Studies in Sociology of Education, 14*, (1), pp. 35-54.

Green, E. H. (2009a) Corporate features and faith-based academies. *Management in Education,* in press.

Green, E. H. (2009b) Discipline and School Ethos: Exploring Students' Reflections upon Values, Rules and the Bible in a Christian City Technology College. *Ethnography and Education,* in press.

Green, E. H. (2009c) Speaking in parables: The responses of students to a Bible-based ethos in a Christian City Technology College. *Cambridge Journal of Education,* in press.

Green, E. H. (forthcoming) An Ethnographic Study of a City Technology College with a Bible-based Ethos. Unpublished DPhil thesis: University of Oxford.

Hand, M. (2001) Is Religious Education possible? An examination of the logical possibility of teaching for religious understanding without religious belief. Unpublished DPhil thesis. University of Oxford.

Hand, M. (2003) A Philosophical objection to faith schools. *Theory and Research in Education,* 1, (1), pp. 89-99.

Hay, D. & Nye, R. (2006) *The spirit of the child.* Revised Edition. London: Jessica Kingsley. Originally published London: Harper Collins 1998.

Hyde, B. (2008) Weaving the threads of meaning: A characteristic of children's spirituality and its implications for Religious Education. *British Journal of Religious Education,* 30, (3), pp. 235-245.

Jelfs, H. (2008) 'Is it the dance of life, Miss?' An exploration of educational paradigm and pedagogical practice in Church of England schools. Unpublished PhD thesis. University of Bristol.

Jeynes, W. H. (2003) The learning habits of twelfth graders attending religious and non-religious schools. *International Journal of Education and Religion,* 4, pp. 145-167.

Jeynes, W. H. (2004) A meta-analysis: Has the academic impact of religious schools changed over the last twenty years? *Journal of Empirical Theology,* 17, (2), pp. 197-216.

Johnson, H. (2001) Living your values: Exploring the 'hidden' culture of a voluntary-controlled Quaker school.

Journal of Beliefs and Values, 22, (2), pp. 197-208.

Johnson, H. (2002) Three Contrasting Approaches in English Church/Faith Schools: perspectives from headteachers. *International Journal of Children's Spirituality,* 7, pp. 209-219.

Johnson, H. & McCreery, E. (1999) The Church of England head: The responsibility for spiritual development and transmission of tradition in a multi-cultural setting. *International Journal of Children's Spirituality,* 4, (2), pp. 165-170.

Kelly, G. (1955) *Principles of personal construct psychology.* New York: Norton.

Kennedy, A. & Duncan, J. (2006) New Zealand children's spirituality in Catholic schools: Teachers' perspectives. *International Journal of Children's Spirituality,* 11, (2), pp. 281-292.

King, U. (2009) *The search for spirituality: Our global quest for meaning and fulfilment.* Canterbury: Canterbury Press.

Kirby, R. (2004) Spirituality and behaviour in school. Bloxham: Bloxham Project.

Lankshear, D. W. (2005) The influence of Anglican secondary schools on personal, moral and religious values. In L.J. Francis, M. Robbins & J. Astley (eds) *Religion, education and adolescence.* Cardiff: University of Wales Press, pp. 55-69.

Mason, M. (2003) Religion and school: A human rights based approach. *British Journal of Religious Education,* 25, (2), pp. 117-128.

Mason, M. (2005) Religion and schools – a fresh way forward? A rights-based approach to diversity in schools. In R. Gardner, J. Cairns & D. Lawton (eds) *Faith schools consensus or conflict.* Abingdon: RoutledgeFalmer, pp. 74-82.

McLaughlin, D. (2005) The dialectic of Australian Catholic education. *International Journal of Children's Spirituality,* 10, (2), pp. 215-233.

McLaughlin, T. (2005) The educative importance of ethos. *British Journal of Educational Studies,* 53, (3), pp. 306-325.

Morris, A. (1998a) Catholic and other secondary schools: An analysis of OfSTED inspection reports, 1993-1995. *Educational Research,* 40, (2), pp. 181-190.

Morris, A. (1998b) So far, so good: Levels of academic achievement in Catholic schools. *Educational Studies,* 24, (1), pp. 83-94.

Morris, A. (2005) Academic standards in Catholic education in England: Indications of causality. *London Review of Education,* 3, (1), pp. 81-99.

Morris, A. (2007) Post-16 pupil performance in Catholic secondary schools in England 1996-2001. *Educational Review,* 59, (1), pp. 55-69.

Morris, A. & Godfrey, R. (2006) A statistical survey of attainment in Catholic schools in England with particular reference to secondary schools operating under the trust deed of the archdiocese of Birmingham. Canterbury: National Institute for Christian Education Research.

National Society For Promoting Religious Education (2007) *Christian character: A handbook for developing an Anglican ethos in independent schools.* [Online] National Society For Promoting Religious Education. Available from: < http://www.natsoc.org.uk/downloads/chrchar/christiancharacter.pdf. > (Accessed 9 May, 2009).

One Hundred and Seventh Congress of the United States of America (2001) No child left behind act. [Online] U.S. Department of Education. Available from: < http://www.ed.gov/nclb/landing.jhtml > (Accessed 9 May, 2009).

Ouseley, H. (2001) Community pride not prejudice. Bradford: Bradford Vision.

Paton, G. (2007) Pupils who flout uniform rules can be sent home. *The Daily Telegraph.* London.

Pennell, H., West, A. & Hind, A. (2007) Religious composition and admission processes of religious schools in London. [Online] Education Research Group, Department of Social Policy, London School of Economics and Political Science. Available from: < http://www.lse.ac.uk/collections/pressAndInformationOffice/newsAndEvents//archives/2007/FaithSchools.htm > (Accessed 9 May, 2009).

Pike, M. A (2004) The challenge of Christian schooling in a secular society. *Journal of Research on Christian Education,* 13, (2) pp. 149-166.

Pike, M. A (2009) The Emmanuel Schools Foundation: Sponsoring and leading transformation at England's most improved academy. *Management in Education,* pp.139-143.

Pring, R. (2005) Are faith schools justified? In R. Gardner, J. Cairns & D. Lawton (eds) *Faith schools consensus or conflict*. Abingdon: RoutledgeFalmer, pp. 51-60.

Pugh, G. & Telhaj, S. (2008) Faith schools, social capital and academic attainment: Evidence from TIMSS-R mathematics scores in Flemish secondary schools. *British Educational Research Journal,* 34**,** (2), pp. 135-268.

Schagen, I. & Schagen, S. (2005) *Combining multilevel analysis with national value – added data sets – a case study to explore the effects of school diversity*. Slough: National Foundation for Education Research.

Schagen, S., Davies, D., Rudd, P. & Schagen, I. (2002a) Impact of specialist and faith schools (LGA Research Report 28). Slough: National Foundation for Education Research.

Schagen, S., Davies, D., Rudd, P. & Schagen, I. (2002b) *The impact of specialist and faith schools in performance*. Slough: National Foundation for Education Research.

Smith, D. (2000) Secularism, religion and education. *Journal of Beliefs and Values,* 21**,** (1), pp. 27-38.

Street, R. W. (2007) The impact of The Way Ahead on headteachers of Anglican voluntary-aided secondary schools. *Journal of Beliefs & Values,* 28, (2), pp. 137-150.

Sultmann, W., Thurgood, G. & Rasmussen, B. (2003) What parents are thinking: some reflections for choices for schooling. *Catholic School Studies,* 76.

Teddlie, C. & Reynolds, D. (2000) *The International handbook of school effectiveness research*. London: Falmer.

Thiessen, E. J. (1993) *Teaching for commitment: Liberal education, indoctrination & Christian nurture*. Leominster: Gracewing.

Tomlinson, S. (2001) *Education in a post-welfare society*. Buckingham: Open University Press.

Toynbee, P. (2006) This is a Clash of Civilisations – Between Reason and Superstition. [Online] *Guardian*. Available from: < http://education.guardian.co.uk/schools/comment/story/0,,1753745,00.html > (Accessed 26 September, 2006).

Treasury (2003) *Every child matters*. Norwich: Stationery Office.

Troyna, B. & Hatcher, R. (1992) *Racism in childrens' lives. A study of mainly white primary schools*. London: Routledge in association with the National Childrens' Bureau.

Twelves, J. (2001) Some characteristics of successful Christian schooling in Australia. *Journal of Education and Christian Belief,* 5, (1), pp. 61-73.

Uecker, J. (2008) Alternative schooling strategies and the religious lives of American adolescents. *Journal for the Scientific Study of Religious Belief,* 47**,** pp. 563-584.

Walford, G. (1991) The reluctant private sector: Of small schools, politics and people. In G. Walford (ed.) *Private Schooling: Tradition, change and diversity*. London: Paul Chapman, pp. 115-132.

Walford, G. (1995) *Educational politics: Pressure groups and faith-based schools*. Aldershot, Avebury: Ashgate Publishing.

Walford, G. (2001) Evangelical Christian schools in the Netherlands. *Oxford Review of Education,* 27, (4), pp. 529-541.

appendix 1: criteria for selection

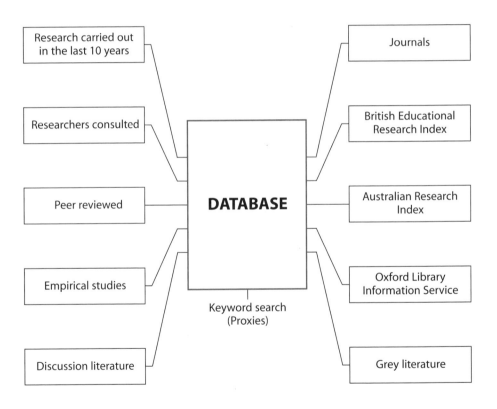

Research carried out in the last 10 years		Journals
Researchers consulted	**DATABASE**	British Educational Research Index
Peer reviewed		Australian Research Index
Empirical studies		Oxford Library Information Service
Discussion literature	Keyword search (Proxies)	Grey literature

AUTHOR & DATE	SHORT TITLE	KEYWORD
GREEN, E. H. (forthcoming)	An ethnographic study of a city technology college with a bible-based ethos.	Academies
GREEN, E. H. (2009)	Corporate features and faith-based Academies.	Academies
GREEN, E. H. (2009)	Discipline and School Ethos: Exploring Pupils' Reflections upon Values, Rules and the Bible in a Christian City Technology College.	Academies
GREEN, E. H. (2009)	Speaking in parables: The responses of pupils to a Bible-based ethos in a Christian City Technology College.	Academies
PIKE, M. A. (2009)	Sponsoring and leading transformation at England's most improved academies.	Academies
GODFREY, R. & MORRIS, A. (2008)	Explaining high attainment in faith schools.	Attainment
JEYNES, W. H. (2003)	The Learning Habits of Twelfth Graders Attending Religious and Non-Religious Schools.	Attainment
JEYNES, W. H. (2004)	A meta analysis: Has the academic impact of religious schools changed over the last twenty years?	Attainment
MORRIS, A. (1997)	Academic and religious outcomes from different models of Catholic schooling.	Attainment
MORRIS, A. (1998)	An analysis of OFSTED inspection reports, 1993-1995.	Attainment
MORRIS, A. (1998)	Levels of academic achievement in Catholic schools.	Attainment
MORRIS, A. (2005)	Academic standards in Catholic education in England.	Attainment
MORRIS, A. (2005)	Diversity, deprivation and the common good.	Attainment
MORRIS, A. (2007)	Post-16 pupil performance in Catholic secondary schools.	Attainment
PUGH, G. & TELHAJ, S. (2008)	Faith schools, social capital and academic attainment.	Attainment
SCHAGEN, S., DAVIES, D., RUDD, P. & SCHAGEN, I. (2002)	Impact of specialist and faith schools.	Attainment
FRANCIS, L. J. (2001)	Religion and Values.	Attitude
FRANCIS, L. J. (2001)	The values debate: A voice from the pupils.	Attitude
FRANCIS, L. J. (2005)	Urban hope and spiritual health: The adolescent voice.	Attitude
FRANCIS, L. J. & JEWELL, A. (1992)	Shaping adolescent attitude towards the church.	Attitude
FRANCIS, L. J. (2005)	Independent Christian schools and pupil values.	Attitude
FRANCIS, L. J. & ROBBINS, M. (2008)	The relationship between denominational affiliation and spiritual health among weekly-churchgoing 13- to 15-year-old adolescents in England and Wales.	Attitude

LANKSHEAR, D. W. (2005)	The Influence of Anglican Secondary Schools on Personal, Moral and Religious Values.	Attitude
ACHESON, B. (2003)	Choruses From The Rock: Developing SQ, Chaplaincy Papers.	Bloxham
ADAMS, A. (2004)	Ruminations of faith in Leadership.	
ARTHUR, J., DEAKIN-CRICK, R., SAMUEL, E., WILSON, K. & MCGETTRICK, B. (2006)	Character education: The formation of virtues and dispositions in 16-19 year olds.	Bloxham
BRYK, A., LEE, V. & HOLLAND, P. (1993)	Catholic schools and the common good.	Catholic
CHANEY, M (2008)	Reflections on some governance challenges.	Catholic
COLSON, I. (2004)	The communication and definition of values in four aided Church of England secondary schools.	Catholic
CURRAN, M. & FRANCIS, L. J. (1996)	Measuring 'Catholic identity' among pupils in Catholic secondary school.	Catholic
DEAKIN CRICK, R. (2002)	Integrating faith and learning.	Catholic
DIXON, R. (2004)	Acceptance of key Catholic beliefs and moral teachings by Generation X Mass attenders.	Catholic
FRANCIS, L. J. (2005)	Urban hope and spiritual health: The adolescent voice.	Catholic
FLYNN, M. & MOK, M. (2000)	Catholic schools 2000: A longitudinal study of Year 12 students in Catholic schools.	Catholic
GODFREY, R. & MORRIS, A. (2008)	Explaining high attainment in faith schools.	Catholic
GRACE, G. (2002)	Catholic schools: Mission, markets and morality.	Catholic
GRACE, G. (2003)	Class, inequality, and Catholic schooling in contemporary contexts.	Catholic
MCLAUGHLIN, D. (2005)	The dialectic of Australian Catholic education.	Catholic
MERCER, G. (2004)	Chairman's address. Catholic Independent Schools' Conference.	Catholic
MORRIS, A. (1997)	Academic and religious outcomes from different models of Catholic schooling.	Catholic
MORRIS, A. (1998)	An analysis of OFSTED inspection reports, 1993-1995.	Catholic
MORRIS, A. (1998)	Levels of academic achievement in Catholic schools.	Catholic
MORRIS, A. (2005)	Academic standards in Catholic education in England.	Catholic
MORRIS, A. (2005)	Diversity, deprivation and the common good.	Catholic
MORRIS, A. (2007)	Post-16 pupil performance in Catholic secondary schools.	Catholic
MORRIS, A. & GODFREY, R. (2006)	A statistical survey of attainment in Catholic schools in England.	Catholic
SUTMANN, W., THURGOOD, G. & RASMUSSEN, B. (2003)	What parents are thinking: Some reflections for choices for schooling.	Catholic
ARTHUR, J. (2009)	Church of England schools research: Values and character dispositions of 14 - 16 year olds.	Catholic
ARTHUR, J., DEAKIN-CRICK, R., SAMUEL, E., WILSON, K. & MCGETTRICK, B. (2006)	Character education: The formation of virtues and dispositions in 16-19 year olds.	Character values education

COLSON, I. (2004)	'Their churches are at home': The communication and definition of values in four aided Church of England secondary schools.	Character values education
DEAKIN CRICK, R. (2002)	Integrating faith and learning.	Character values education
JELFS, H. (2008)	An exploration of educational paradigm and pedagogical practice in Church of England schools.	Character values education
JOHNSON, H. (2001)	Living Your Values: Exploring the 'hidden' culture of a voluntary-controlled Quaker school.	Character values education
ARTHUR, J. (2003)	Education with character.	Character values education
BADLEY, K. (1998)	Identifying Christian Schools.	Christian Education (discussion)
COOLING, T. (2007)	The challenge of passionate religious commitment for school education in a world of religious diversity.	Christian Education (discussion)
PIKE, M. A (2004)	The Challenge of Christian Schooling in a Secular Society.	Christian Education (discussion)
SMITH, D. (2000)	Secularism, Religion and Education.	Christian Education (discussion)
THIESSEN, E. J. (1993)	Teaching for commitment.	Christian Education (discussion)
ARTHUR, J. (2009)	Church of England schools research: Values and character dispositions of 14 - 16 year olds.	Christian Education (discussion)
ARTHUR, J. & GODFREY, R. (2005)	Statistical survey of the attainment and achievement of pupils in Church of England schools.	Church of England
BROWN, A. (2003)	Church of England schools: Politics, power and identity.	Church of England
COLSON, I. (2004)	The communication and definition of values in four aided Church of England secondary schools.	Church of England
DEAKIN CRICK, R. (2002)	Integrating faith and learning: An empirical case study from a Church of England secondary school.	Church of England
DEARING, R. (2001)	The Way Ahead.	Church of England
FRANCIS, L. J. (2005)	Urban hope and spiritual health: The adolescent voice.	Church of England
FRANCIS, L. J. & JEWELL, A. (1992)	Shaping adolescent attitude towards the church: Comparison between Church of England and county secondary schools.	Church of England
GAY, B. (2000)	Fostering Spiritual Development through the Religious Dimension of Schools: The report of a pilot study in 17 independent schools.	Church of England
GILL, J. (2004)	The act of collective worship: Pupils' perspectives.	Church of England
GODFREY, R. (2009)	Godfrey, R. (2009) Faith schools and socio-economic deprivation: a statistical enquiry.	Church of England
JELFS, H. (2008)	An exploration of educational paradigm and pedagogical practice in Church of England schools.	Church of England
JOHNSON, H. (2002)	Three Contrasting Approaches in English Church/Faith Schools: Perspectives from headteachers.	Church of England
JOHNSON, H. & MCCREERY, E.	The Church of England Head: The responsibility for spiritual development and transmission of tradition in a multi-cultural setting.	Church of England
LANKSHEAR, D. W. (2005)	The Influence of Anglican Secondary Schools on Personal, Moral and Religious Values.	Church of England

NATIONAL SOCIETY FOR PROMOTING RELIGIOUS EDUCATION (2007)	Christian character: A handbook for developing an Anglican ethos in independent schools.	Church of England
STREET, R. W. (2007)	The impact of the Way Ahead on headteachers of Anglican voluntary-aided secondary schools.	Church of England
DAVIES, G. (2007)	Spiritual development in church schools: a survey of Welsh headteachers' perceptions.	Church of Wales
DAVIES, G. & FRANCIS, L. J. (2007)	Three approaches to Religious Education at Key Stages One and Two in Wales.	Church of Wales
BERKELY, R. (2008)	The right to divide.	Faith schools
BRITISH HUMANIST ASSOCIATION (2002)	A better way forward.	Faith schools
DCSF (2007)	Faith in the system.	Faith schools
DWYER, J. (1998)	Religious schools versus children's rights.	Faith schools
GIBBONS, S. & SILVA, O. (2006)	Faith primary schools: Better schools or better pupils?	Faith schools
HAND, M. (2001)	Is Religious Education possible?	Faith schools
MASON, M. (2003)	Religion and school: A human rights based approach.	Faith schools
MASON, M. (2005)	Religion and schools – a fresh way forward.	Faith schools
OUSELEY, H. (2001)	Community pride not prejudice.	Faith schools
PENNELL, H., WEST, A. & HIND, A. (2007)	Religious composition and admissions processes of religious schools in London.	Faith schools
PRING, R. (2005)	Are faith schools justified?	Faith schools
SCHAGEN, I. & SCHAGEN, S. (2005)	Combining multilevel analysis with national value-added data sets.	Faith schools
SCHAGEN, S., DAVIES, D., RUDD, P. & SCHAGEN, I. (2002)	The impact of specialist and faith schools in performance.	Faith schools
BLAIN, M. & REVELL, L. (2002)	Patterns of Spiritual and Moral Development in Religious and Public Schools in Chicago.	International
BRYK, A., LEE, V. & HOLLAND, P. (1993)	Catholic schools and the common good.	International
CHANEY, M. (2008)	Reflections on some governance challenges.	International
COLLIER, J. & DOWSON, M. (2007)	Applying an action research approach to improving the quality of Christian education.	International
DE ROOS, S. A., IEDEMA, J. & MIEDEMA, S. (2003)	Effects of Mothers' and Schools' Religious Denomination on Preschool Children's God Concepts.	International
DE WOLFF, A. J. C., DE RUYTER, D. J. & MIEDEMA, S. (2003)	Being a Christian school in the Netherlands.	International
DRIESSEN, G. W. J. M. (2002)	The effect of religious groups' dominance in classrooms on cognitive and noncognitive educational outcomes.	International
DONNELLY, C. (2000)	In pursuit of school ethos.	International
DONNELLY, C. (2008)	The integrated school in a conflict society.	International
FISHER, J. (1999)	Helps to fostering pupils' spiritual health.	International

FISHER, J. (2004)	Feeling good, living life: A spiritual health measure for young children.	International
FISHER, J. (2008)	Impacting teachers' and pupils' spiritual well-being.	International
FISHER, J., FRANCIS, L. J. & JOHNSON, P. (2000)	Assessing spiritual health via four domains of well-being.	International
FRANCIS, L. J., ROBBINS, M., BARNES, P. & LEWIS, C. (2006)	Religiously affiliated schools in Northern Ireland.	International
GLENN, C. & DE GROOF, J. (2002)	Finding the right balance: Freedom, autonomy and accountability in education.	International
HYDE, B. (2008)	Weaving the threads of meaning: A characteristic of children's spirituality and its implications for Religious Education.	International
JEYNES, W. H. (2003)	The Learning Habits of Twelfth Graders Attending Religious and Non-Religious School.	International
KENNEDY, A. & DUNCAN, J. (2006)	New Zealand children's spirituality in Catholic schools: Teachers' perspectives.	International
MCLAUGHLIN, D. (2005)	The dialectic of Australian Catholic education.	International
PUGH, G. & TELHAJ, S. (2008)	Faith schools, social capital and academic attainment.	International
SUTMANN, W., THURGOOD, G. & RASMUSSEN, B. (2003)	What parents are thinking: Some reflections for choices for schooling.	International
UECKER, J. (2008)	Alternative schooling strategies and the religious lives of American adolescents.	International
WALFORD, G. (2001)	Evangelical Christian schools in the Netherlands.	International
AP SION, T., FRANCIS, L. J. & BAKER, S. (2007)	Experiencing education in the new Christian schools in the United Kingdom: Listening to the male graduates.	New Christian Schools
BAKER, S. & FREEMAN, D. (2005)	The love of God in the classroom.	New Christian Schools
DEAKIN, R. (1989)	The new Christian schools.	New Christian Schools
FRANCIS, L. J. (2005)	Urban hope and spiritual health: The adolescent voice.	New Christian Schools
FRANCIS, L. J. (2005)	Independent Christian schools and pupil values.	New Christian Schools
FRANCIS, L. J., AP SION, T. & BAKER, S. (2009)	The theological case for Christian schools in England and Wales.	New Christian Schools
GREEN, E. H. (forthcoming)	An ethnographic study of a city technology college with a bible-based ethos.	New Christian Schools
GREEN, E. H. (2009)	Corporate features and faith-based Academies.	New Christian Schools
GREEN, E. H. (2009)	Discipline and School Ethos: Exploring Pupils' Reflections upon Values, Rules and the Bible in a Christian City Technology College.	New Christian Schools
GREEN, E. H. (2009)	Speaking in parables: The responses of pupils to a Bible-based ethos in a Christian City Technology College.	New Christian Schools
PIKE, M. A. (2009)	Sponsoring and leading transformation at England's most improved academies.	New Christian Schools
WALFORD, G. (1991)	The reluctant private sector.	New Christian Schools

WALFORD, G. (1995)	Educational politics: Pressure groups and faith-based schools.	New Christian Schools
BLOXHAM PROJECT (2007)	The spiritual dimension of school leadership.	Private Schools
BLOXHAM PROJECT (2008)	Youth spirituality.	Private Schools
NATIONAL SOCIETY FOR PROMOTING RELIGIOUS EDUCATION (2007)	Christian character: A handbook for developing an Anglican ethos in independent schools.	Private Schools
GAY, B. (2000)	Fostering Spiritual Development through the Religious Dimension of Schools: The report of a pilot study in 17 independent schools.	Private Schools
WALFORD, G. (1991)	The reluctant private sector.	Private Schools
BLAIN, M. & REVELL, L. (2002)	Patterns of Spiritual and Moral Development in Religious and Public Schools in Chicago.	Religious identity spiritual development
BLOXHAM PROJECT (2007)	The spiritual dimension of school leadership.	Religious identity spiritual development
BLOXHAM PROJECT (2008)	Youth spirituality.	Religious identity spiritual development
DAVIES, G. (2007)	Spiritual development in church schools a survey of Welsh headteachers' perceptions.	Religious identity spiritual development
DE WOLFF, A. J. C., DE RUYTER, D. J. & MIEDEMA, S. (2003)	Being a Christian school in the Netherlands: An analysis of 'identity' conceptions and their practical implications.	Religious identity spiritual development
ERRICKER, C. (2007)	Children's spirituality and post-modern faith.	Religious identity spiritual development
FISHER, J. W. (2004)	Feeling good, living life: A spiritual health measure for young children.	Religious identity spiritual development
FISHER, J. W. (2006)	Using secondary pupils' views about influences on their spiritual well-being to inform pastoral care.	Religious identity spiritual development
FISHER, J. W., FRANCIS, L. J. & JOHNSON, P. (2000)	Assessing spiritual health via four domains of well-being.	Religious identity spiritual development
FLYNN, M. & MOK, M. (2000)	Catholic schools 2000: A longitudinal study of Year 12 students in Catholic schools.	Religious identity spiritual development
GAY, B. (2000)	Fostering Spiritual Development through the Religious Dimension of Schools: The report of a pilot study in 17 independent schools.	Religious identity spiritual development
HAY, D. & NYE, R. (2006)	The Spirit of the Child.	Religious identity spiritual development
HYDE, B. (2008)	Weaving the threads of meaning.	Religious identity spiritual development
KENNEDY, A. & DUNCAN, J. (2006)	New Zealand children's spirituality in Catholic schools: Teachers' perspectives.	Religious identity spiritual development
KIRBY, R. (2004)	Spirituality and Behaviour in School.	Religious identity spiritual development

**DEFINITIONS OF
CHRISTIAN ETHOS SCHOOLS**

Types in the literature

UK	**INTERNATIONAL**
Maintained Church Schools	Maintained Church schools
Traditional Independent Schools (Christian Foundation)	Independent Church schools
New Christian Schools	Subsidised Christian schools
Sponsored Academies, CTCs and specialist schools	

DEFINITION OF IMPACT

These stem from different research paradigms in the literature

Belief	Attitudes	Behaviours	Spiritual Development
ethnographic case study research	survey design questionnaires	statistical (often research into attainment)	survey design spiritual health